THE GREAT NAVY BIRDS OF LAKE MICHIGAN

THE GREAT NAVY BIRDS OF LAKE MICHIGAN

The True Story of the Privateers of Lake Michigan and the Aircraft They Rescued

TARAS C. LYSSENKO

AMERICA
THROUGH
TIME

America Through Time is an imprint of Sutton Publishing Inc
www.through-time.com
office@through-time.com

First published 2019
Reprinted 2025

ISBN 978-1-63499-143-8

Typeset in 10pt on 13pt Sabon
Printed and bound in England

Foreword

I served as the Director of the National Naval Aviation Museum from 1986 until 2014. In my first few years as director, I was not particularly interested in or even aware of the amazing source of historic naval aircraft that existed under water. I was fairly convinced that there were no World War II and earlier naval aircraft left that had not already been claimed. Those claimed were not by the Naval Aviation Museum. In fact, it became very obvious that, with some rare exceptions, mostly through the Smithsonian Air and Space Museum, there were practically none of the tens of thousands of aircraft produced for or by the Navy since its aviation inception in 1910 that had been saved for historic purposes. Then I came across a museum memo to the Naval Air Systems Command, at the time the "owner" of all aircraft built for the Navy, wherever they might be. Written by my predecessor, the memo declared that the Naval Aviation Museum was not interested in any submerged aircraft of any kind. It was composed to reject involvement in the recovery of World War II Navy aircraft submerged in Lake Michigan, which were being pursued by two museums on the East Coast. I immediately rescinded the memo, but it was too late, the two aircraft had already been handed over on loan to the museums for recovery. At about the same time, several other things happened that piqued my interest in underwater aircraft.

One thing was a report from the Navy Superintendent of Salvage that they had discovered a nearly intact bi-wing aircraft sitting on its nose at the bottom of the Pacific Ocean off of Del Mar, California. They were proposing recovery and delivery to an interested museum. Ours was definitely that interested museum, and I immediately made arrangements to have the aircraft, a F3F Grumman fighter, assigned to us. We then secured a relatively small amount of funding from the Navy to support the recovery. It was an interesting evolution, including inputs from "experts" in metal deterioration who insisted that the aircraft, having been under salt water for some forty-nine years, would completely disintegrate once the attempt to pull it from the bottom began. We "non-experts" forged ahead nevertheless. The recovery was successful, and with the exception of some magnesium parts, the experts were dead wrong. There was little major structural deterioration from the prolonged salt water exposure. The aircraft, thanks to restoration efforts by artisans at the San Diego Air & Space Museum, sits fully restored on our museum floor. It is still not deteriorating as a result of its long exposure.

The second thing I was soon to learn was a rather unusual proposal—one highly unlikly to succeed. A former naval aviator and brand-new law school graduate came to me and explained that he knew of the location of the carcass of a SBD Dauntless in Lake Michigan that he would like to try to recover for the museum. Of course, he needed financial support. Despite his total inexperience in the field, he eventually did receive my support and that of the Naval Aviation Museum Foundation with a small grant to give it a try. To everyone's amazement, he succeeded and our adventure with the Lake Michigan treasure of historic naval aircraft began. However, it was not with our new lawyer friend, who had declared himself done with that line of work, but with a little known company from Chicago calling itself A and T Recovery.

A and T Recovery had recovered the aircraft for the East Coast museum and wanted to retrieve more for us. We were enthusiatically willing, but unfortunately unable since there was no funding available to hire A and T Recovery to do the work. The public law we had to use to acquire artifacts through trade of Navy surplus material for like items from the civilian sector would not help. Salvaging aircraft was not a "like item." The district Congressional Representative for the Pensacola area, a strong military supporter, came to the rescue. He had the law modified to include services, such as artifact recovery and restoration/preservation. We were in business and so was A and T Recovery. This book is largely focused on the Naval Aviation Museum/Naval Aviation Museum Foundation/A and T Recovery partnership that ensued.

Over the next nearly thirty years, we were able to initiate and fulfill contracts for aircraft recovery through the rewritten law. The service provided was the discovery and recovery of dozens of aircraft from the bottom of Lake Michigan, which has immeasurably benefitted the National Naval Aviation Museum. Additonally, the benefit extended well beyond the Naval Aviation Museum. Numerous other museums and venues around the country are displaying one or more of these aircraft, which are now on loan from the Naval Aviation Museum. Included in these recipients are the National Museum of the Marine Corps, the National World War II Museum, the San Diego Air & Space Museum, the Kalamazoo Aviation History Museum, and numerous other locations across the country. All but the two aircraft mentioned earlier were discovered and recovered by A and T Recovey. These priceless recoveries were accomplished at essentially zero monetary cost to the Navy.

The result was the acquisition of priceless examples of aircraft from World War II that did not previously exist for display by the Navy and other important venues. A SBD Dauntless that is the only remaining survivor of the Battle of Midway, three other combat service SBDs, and a F6F-3 Hellcat that saw action in the Solomon Islands were added to the Navy's historic collection when no other such veterans had existed. We also added several Grumman-built Wildcat fighters, none had been saved after the war. Additionally, we located, recovered, and restored the only known to exist Vought SB2U Vindicator and an extremely rare F4U-1 "Birdcage" Corsair. These and the other examples serve to display and preserve aircraft that otherwise would be lost to history by the eventual deterioration of artifacts left at the bottom of bodies of water.

On occasion, I have been asked why I dealt almost exclusively with A and T Recovery, or for that matter, why I dealt with them at all given their sometimes politically incorrect approach to dealing with government bureaucracies. "Why in the world do you deal with these guys? After all, there are any number of other entities that would be willing and have offered to sweep the bottom of Lake Michigan for these aircraft." My answer is a simple one: the owners of A and T Recovery are honest, candid, persistant, and innovative. More importantly, they produce, unconditionally, on schedule, on budget, and without loss or damage of any kind in their search and recovery operations. In my experience, no other entity had been able to display such capabilities.

The enrichment of the story of naval aviation represented by the discovery and recovery of these lost artifacts of our history would likely never have happened without the dynamic and highly effective involvement of A and T Recovery. It was their relationship with the National Naval Aviation Museum and the Naval Aviation Museum Foundation that made the effort to fill the gaps in the Navy's historic aviation collection a resounding success. The story of this effort is well worth telling.

Captain Robert Rasmussen
U.S.N. (Ret.)

Contents

Preface

There are times in life when people tell stories that are truly unbelievable. With this book, I am going to tell one such tale. Actually, I am going to tell a lot of stories that combine to form a fable that has taken place over the past seventy-five years. However, what is in this anthology is completely honest and true.

As with all good stories, it involves many people. There are conflicts between good and bad. In this story, there are protagonists, villains, and outright antagonists. What is different is that the story tells that with the support of hundreds, if not thousands of people working together, great and wondrous things can be achieved. We should never give up at trying to make the world a better place, no matter who attempts to interfere.

1

The Project that Set Everything in Motion

Aircraft carriers on Lake Michigan?

In 1941, war raged across the world. Nazi Germany controlled vast swaths of Europe and Northern Africa. Imperial Japan occupied the countries of Vietnam, Laos, Cambodia, extensive territory in mainland China, and would soon seize Thailand, Malaysia, the Philippines, Burma, and others. In the United States of America, there was a prevalent attitude to remain neutral: it was "their" war, not ours. Countries such as Great Britain, Australia, and New Zealand were in grave danger, about to face great onslaughts from methods of warfare that had undergone changes since the end of the Great War.

Armies were now extremely mobile, with mechanized tanks and troop carriers supported by aircraft that could precision target and bomb opposing forces. On the oceans, the age of the "dreadnought" was ending. Waters across the globe were prowled by the undersea boat, and the aircraft carrier was quickly becoming the purveyor of the projection of military might. On December 7, 1941, the Japanese Imperial Navy demonstrated the effectiveness of the aircraft carrier by attacking the U.S Navy at Pearl Harbor, Hawaii. The Imperial Navy launched two waves of approximately 350 aircraft from six aircraft carriers. The attack devastated the American Pacific battleship fleet, bringing the total destruction of U.S.S. *Oklahoma* and U.S.S. *Arizona*, as well as sinking or damaging six others, including several cruisers and destroyers. The ill-prepared U.S. Navy escaped far worse impact because its aircraft carriers were not present in the harbor at the time.

Although the attack was a great tactical success, its strategic outcome was that of monumental motivation and activation of the industrial and military might of the U.S: the War Department went into full operation; enlistments in all branches of the armed forces swelled to levels never seen before; automotive and other large manufacturers shifted their production assembly lines to the building of trucks, tanks, boats, and aircraft; youth scoured the country for scrap metals in order to meet growing material demands; and adults planted "victory" gardens to boost food production. An entire nation of over 100 million mobilized to bring forth a unified force, *e pluribus unum*, in order to defeat the Axis forces of Europe and Asia.

In the middle of all these efforts, a plan was devised to train and qualify Navy aircraft carrier pilots far from the American coasts, in a place where German U-boats and Japanese submarines would not be able to find training carriers for easy target practice. Chicago, on the southwestern shore of Lake Michigan, with its close proximity to Great Lakes Naval Training Station and the essential Glenview Naval Air Station, was selected. Two former Great Lakes steam-powered side-paddle wheel excursion vessels, the S.S. *See and Bee* and the S.S. *Greater Buffalo*, were purchased and converted into make-shift flattops. The first ship, the U.S.S. *Wolverine*, began qualifications of aircraft carrier pilots of the U.S. Navy and its allies in October 1942. The U.S.S. *Sable* came soon after. Over the next three years, nearly 15,000 pilots and great numbers of deck crews would be qualified and trained to go on to achieve victory in the air war and support the ground campaigns in the pacific.

During the Lake Michigan carrier operations, approximately 130 aircraft were lost in the lake. The operations resulted in approximately a dozen pilots losing their lives, and with the program operating throughout the year, many of these deaths were a result of exposure. The lost aircraft included several dozen Grumman TBF Avenger torpedo-bombers, many Douglas SBD Dauntless dive-bombers, a lot of Grumman-built and designed F4F/FM (General Motors) Wildcat fighters, a Vought SB2U Vindicator scout-bomber, a Grumman F6F-3 Hellcat fighter, a Vought F4U-1 "Bird Cage" Corsair fighter, and a number of North American T-6/SNJ Texan Trainers. These aircraft seemed to be lost to time until the late 1970s, when the height of interest in self-contained underwater breathing apparatuses and the exploration of marine environments, at which point several of the aircraft were located. That is when A and T Recovery's involvement in this story began.

A and T Recovery, which stands for Allan Olson and Taras Lyssenko Recovery, started as a group of boys from the near west Chicago suburb of Berwyn, Illinois. There were about ten of us when we began. Al bought an old boat that seemed to be held together with duct tape and was far from safe for use on Lake Michigan, but we were young, dumb, and invincible. We started looking for the many shipwrecks that had been lost over the nearly century and half that Chicago was a busy marine port. Learning of the World War II aircraft, we shifted our attention in their direction. Soon, Al and I located a badly damaged Wildcat Fighter, which we turned over to marine salvage operators, who recovered her for a private collector.

Most of the group matured and went on to other endeavors, such as marriage and the rearing of offspring. Al and I became distracted for several years with college and military service, but returned to the lake *circa* 1986. We purchased a sizeable sport fishing cabin cruiser-style boat and quickly modified it for survey and salvage operations. Additionally, we purchased the most important technology, from my point of view, used in marine exploration—a side-scan sonar, an EG&G Model 259-4. We were off and running, or perhaps swimming. Soon thereafter, others, such as Keith Pearson, who were extremely interested in the lost aircraft, joined the team, rounding out what was a somewhat of a ragtag crew with a lot energy and determination.

There has always been a misconception that there are some members of a branch of the U.S. Navy who know or knew where the lost aircraft were located. Perhaps the staff of Naval Historical Center, now known as the Naval History and Heritage Command, but that is a fallacy. During the training operations, the two ships used a

S.S. *See and Bee* being converted into U.S.S. *Wolverine* (IX-64) at Buffalo, New York, in early 1942. Note on the bow of the ship that its name is written as "C & B." (*Courtesy of C. C. Wright*)

U.S.S. *Wolverine* (IX-64) being converted from S.S. *See and Bee* at Buffalo, New York, on June 12, 1942.

U.S.S. *Wolverine* (IX-64) at Buffalo, New York, in early 1942 just after completion. At left is the stern of S.S. *Greater Buffalo*, just beginning conversion to U.S.S. *Sable* (IX-81). (*Courtesy of C. C. Wright*)

U.S.S. *Sable* (IX-81) fitting out at Buffalo, New York, January 15, 1943, during conversion from S.S. *Greater Buffalo*. (*Courtesy of C. C. Wright*).

U.S.S. *Sable* (IX-81) moored in an icy Great Lakes harbor on May 8, 1943, the day she was placed in commission. The location may be Buffalo, New York, where she was converted from the side-wheel excursion steamship *Greater Buffalo*. (*Official U.S. Navy Photograph, now in the collections of the National Archives*)

A General Motors FM-2 Wildcat fighter upended after a barrier crash on board U.S.S. *Sable* (IX-81), during pilot training on Lake Michigan, May 1945. Another FM-2 is flying past in top center. (*Official U.S. Navy Photograph, now in the collections of the National Archives*)

The Carrier Qualification Training Unit Insignia emblem from the Great Lakes that was in use 1942–43. The ship in the design is the U.S.S. *Wolverine* (IX-64).

new technology, for the era, called radar. In general, when there was an accident where an aircraft went into the water, the position of ship would be recorded in the "deck log" with the distance and an azimuth to known locations. Common locations would be the Chicago harbor entrance lighthouse or the harbor entrance at Waukegan, Illinois. The deck logs of the U.S.S. *Wolverine* and the U.S.S. *Sable* were held in the U.S. National Archives, Washington, D.C. Al and I, along with my two brothers, Alexander and Scott, took turns going to the archives where we read though every single page of the deck logs. We recorded the position data and photographed what we read. Several years later, the National Archives transferred all ships' deck logs to microfilm. We gathered a lot of other important information with the assistance of an archivist, Barry Zerby, who knew the U.S. Naval records inside-out. We then took all that data and charted the indicated aircraft positions as starting points for what would become years of side-scan surveys.

At the time, there was a very strong interest in military history, especially in the weapon systems of World War II. The aircraft were highly prized for, so many other examples of them had been destroyed at the end of the war. There were very wealthy collectors and museums that were willing to invest large amounts of money to locate, retrieve, and restore the aircraft, many to their original flying condition. These people sent teams to search and recover aircraft from all the places the war had been fought, from the islands and jungles of Southeast Asia to the tundra of the former U.S.S.R. The lost aircraft of Lake Michigan had caught the attention of many of these people. However, there was a problem for everyone that sought aircraft from Lake Michigan: all of the aircraft are owned by the U.S. Government.

There always seems to be a prevailing belief that if one person searches for and finds something that has been lost underwater, the item becomes the property of the person who finds it. The concept is just not true. I use an analogy that explains who owns most things that have been lost underwater. If a person loses their wallet in the parking lot of

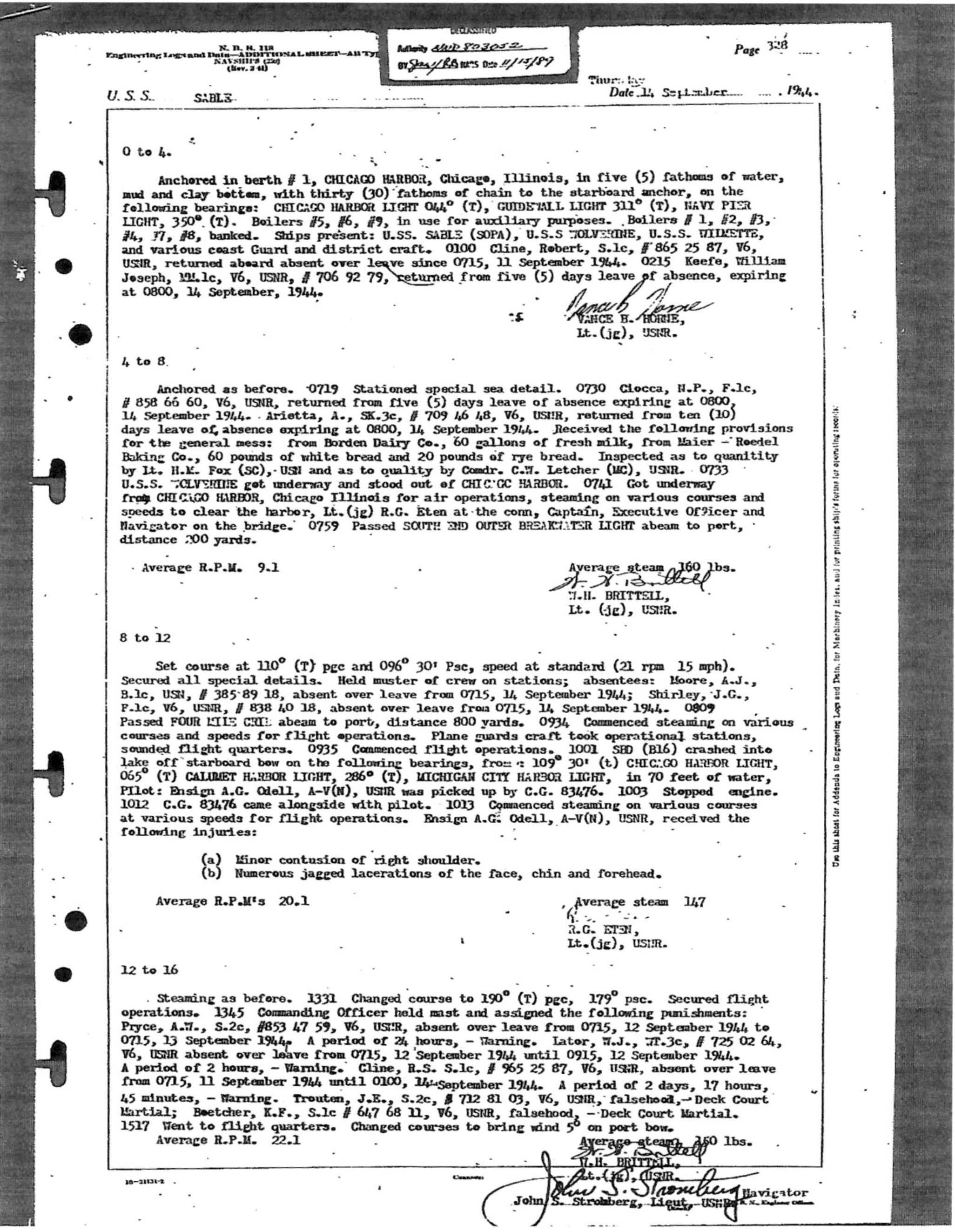

N. D. N. 118
Engineering Log and Data—ADDITIONAL SHEET—AIR TYPE
NAVSHIPS (24)
(Rev. 3-41)

DECLASSIFIED
Authority [illegible]
BY [illegible] Date 11/17/87

Page 328

U. S. S. SABLE

Thursday
Date 14 September 1944.

0 to 4.

Anchored in berth # 1, CHICAGO HARBOR, Chicago, Illinois, in five (5) fathoms of water, mud and clay bottom, with thirty (30) fathoms of chain to the starboard anchor, on the following bearings: CHICAGO HARBOR LIGHT 044° (T), GUIDEWALL LIGHT 311° (T), NAVY PIER LIGHT, 350° (T). Boilers #5, #6, #9, in use for auxiliary purposes. Boilers # 1, #2, #3, #4, #7, #8, banked. Ships present: U.SS. SABLE (SOPA), U.S.S WOLVERINE, U.S.S. WILMETTE, and various coast Guard and district craft. 0100 Cline, Robert, S.1c, # 865 25 87, V6, USNR, returned aboard absent over leave since 0715, 11 September 1944. 0215 Keefe, William Joseph, MM.1c, V6, USNR, # 706 92 79, returned from five (5) days leave of absence, expiring at 0800, 14 September, 1944.

VANCE B. HORNE,
Lt.(jg), USNR.

4 to 8.

Anchored as before. 0719 Stationed special sea detail. 0730 Ciocca, N.P., F.1c, # 858 66 60, V6, USNR, returned from five (5) days leave of absence expiring at 0800, 14 September 1944. Arietta, A., SK.3c, # 709 46 48, V6, USNR, returned from ten (10) days leave of absence expiring at 0800, 14 September 1944. Received the following provisions for the general mess: from Borden Dairy Co., 60 gallons of fresh milk, from Maier - Roedel Baking Co., 60 pounds of white bread and 20 pounds of rye bread. Inspected as to quanitity by Lt. H.M. Fox (SC), USN and as to quality by Comdr. C.W. Letcher (MC), USNR. 0733 U.S.S. WOLVERINE got underway and stood out of CHICAGO HARBOR. 0741 Got underway from CHICAGO HARBOR, Chicago Illinois for air operations, steaming on various courses and speeds to clear the harbor, Lt.(jg) R.G. Eten at the conn, Captain, Executive Officer and Navigator on the bridge. 0759 Passed SOUTH END OUTER BREAKWATER LIGHT abeam to port, distance 200 yards.

Average R.P.M. 9.1 Average steam 160 lbs.

W.H. BRITTELL,
Lt. (jg), USNR.

8 to 12

Set course at 110° (T) pgc and 096° 30' Psc, speed at standard (21 rpm 15 mph). Secured all special details. Held muster of crew on stations; absentees: Moore, A.J., B.1c, USN, # 385 89 18, absent over leave from 0715, 14 September 1944; Shirley, J.G., F.1c, V6, USNR, # 838 40 18, absent over leave from 0715, 14 September 1944. 0809 Passed FOUR MILE CRIB abeam to port, distance 800 yards. 0934 Commenced steaming on various courses and speeds for flight operations. Plane guards craft took operational stations, sounded flight quarters. 0935 Commenced flight operations. 1001 SBD (B16) crashed into lake off starboard bow on the following bearings, from: 109° 30' (t) CHICAGO HARBOR LIGHT, 065° (T) CALUMET HARBOR LIGHT, 286° (T), MICHIGAN CITY HARBOR LIGHT, in 70 feet of water, Pilot: Ensign A.G. Odell, A-V(N), USNR was picked up by C.G. 83476. 1003 Stopped engine. 1012 C.G. 83476 came alongside with pilot. 1013 Commenced steaming on various courses at various speeds for flight operations. Ensign A.G. Odell, A-V(N), USNR, received the following injuries:

(a) Minor contusion of right shoulder.
(b) Numerous jagged lacerations of the face, chin and forehead.

Average R.P.M's 20.1 Average steam 147

R.G. ETEN,
Lt.(jg), USNR.

12 to 16

Steaming as before. 1331 Changed course to 190° (T) pgc, 179° psc. Secured flight operations. 1345 Commanding Officer held mast and assigned the following punishments: Pryce, A.W., S.2c, #853 47 59, V6, USNR, absent over leave from 0715, 12 September 1944 to 0715, 13 September 1944. A period of 24 hours, - Warning. Lator, W.J., WT.3c, # 725 02 64, V6, USNR absent over leave from 0715, 12 September 1944 until 0915, 12 September 1944. A period of 2 hours, - Warning. Cline, R.S. S.1c, # 965 25 87, V6, USNR, absent over leave from 0715, 11 September 1944 until 0100, 14 September 1944. A period of 2 days, 17 hours, 45 minutes, - Warning. Trouten, J.E., S.2c, # 712 81 03, V6, USNR, falsehood, - Deck Court Martial; Beetcher, K.F., S.1c # 647 68 11, V6, USNR, falsehood, - Deck Court Martial. 1517 Went to flight quarters. Changed courses to bring wind 5° on port bow.

Average R.P.M. 22.1 Average steam 160 lbs.

W.H. BRITTELL,
Lt.(jg), USNR.

John S. Stromberg, Lieut., USNR Navigator

Use this sheet for Addenda to Engineering Logs and Data, for Machinery Index, and for printing ship's forms for operating records.

What I would consider a typical log page for one of the days aboard a Lake Michigan "Flat Top." In the center of the page, there is the documentation of the crash of "SBD (16)," 10575. An aircraft that would come to play a substantial role in this story.

a large supermarket and is not able to find it, but another person does, its contents still belong to the person who originally lost it. In modern society, we generally reward those that return items that we have lost. The aircraft of Lake Michigan were lost during the Navy training operation of World War II. They are still property of the U.S. Government no matter how much time, money, and effort any private citizen puts into locating them. Therefore, in order to retrieve any of the aircraft from Lake Michigan, we had to engage their owner.

In the mid-1980s, lost or missing U.S. Navy aircraft were the responsibility of a branch of the Navy, Naval Air Systems Command, "NavAir." NavAir's mission is to provide material support for aircraft and airborne weapon systems for the modern Navy. Missing and lost aircraft of World War II were not very high on their priority list. Al and I realized a way to take advantage of that situation. The Navy has its own museum system to include the National Museum of Naval Aviation, now called the National Naval Aviation Museum. Its director, *circa* 1986, did not have any interest in the Lake Michigan aircraft. Apparently, he felt that aircraft that had been lost for some time underwater were never worth recovery and restoration. Other museum directors felt differently. There was and still is a process where museums outside of the U.S. governmental system can be approved to receive on loan and for public display items that are part of the Navy's historic collection. The museums that wished for us to recover an aircraft from Lake Michigan simply made a formal written request to NavAir. The Command was always very agreeable and granted approval to the museums, to include the Cradle of Aviation Museum, Garden City, New York and Patriots Point Naval & Maritime Museum, Charleston Harbor, South Carolina, home of the U.S.S. *Yorktown*.

In 1987, Captain Robert L. Rasmussen, U.S.N. (Ret.), took the helm as the new director of the National Museum of Naval Aviation. For the four years prior, he had served as the development director of the Naval Aviation Museum Foundation, a 501(c) (3) that at the time supported the efforts to expand and enhance the museum. Captain Rasmussen had taken some time to look at some of the aircraft we had recovered from the lake and he wanted to secure what he could for his museum. Once becoming director, he wasted little time in contacting us at A and T Recovery.

Captain Rasmussen presented us with a very interesting concept. He did not have money—there is nothing in the budget of the U.S. Navy that allows payment for the recovery of once lost World War II aircraft—but what he did have as a tool was a little known section in the U.S. Code, Title 10 U.S. Code § 2572, documents, historical artifacts, and condemned or obsolete combat materiel: loan, gift, or exchange. His idea was, instead of paying us money for our service to locate and recover the aircraft, the Navy would exchange old, used, no longer needed equipment that would otherwise go into the scrap pile or garbage heap. The obsolete items could even include vintage aircraft that private collectors would have a lot of interest in purchasing.

We were in an awkward position that we really were very unfamiliar with. The Captain made it clear to us that we actually had little choice but to entertain his proposal. We would no longer be able to recovery any aircraft for other museums without his consent. He had gone to the Navy's upper command and had them transfer the responsibility for all the lost aircraft from NavAir to whomever was the director of the National Museum of Naval Aviation. He happened to be the director at the time and would be for the next twenty-five years. He now controlled what was to be our future

Preparing to load the F4F-3 Wildcat, 12297, for the Cradle of Aviation Museum just after its rescue by A and T Recovery. (*Photograph courtesy of the Cradle of Aviation Museum*)

The truck loading of the Wildcat for the Cradle of Aviation Museum. (*Photograph courtesy of the Cradle of Aviation Museum*)

F4F-3 Wildcat, 12297, undergoing going metal work restoration by volunteers from Northrup Grumman Aerospace Systems. (*Photograph courtesy of the Cradle of Aviation Museum*)

F4F-3 Wildcat, 12297, on display at the Cradle of Aviation Museum. Aircraft fabric restoration and painting were done by volunteers to/for the Cradle of Aviation Museum. (*Photographs courtesy of the Cradle of Aviation Museum; photographer Rod Leonhard*)

Right: Photograph of Ensign Horace Little, U.S.N.R. Ensign Little crashed with F4F-3 Wildcat, 12297, on January 16, 1944 off U.S.S. *Sable*.

Below: Allan Olson standing on the Wildcat recovered for Patriots Point Naval & Maritime Museum.

Taras Lyssenko sitting in the cockpit of the SBD-5 Dauntless, 36173, recovered for Patriots Point Naval & Maritime Museum.

with the once lost Navy aircraft. However, there was an even greater issue looming. The law required that any exchange had to be what was termed as "like item for like item." In order to receive an obsolete aircraft from the Navy, we had to present an aircraft that we owned for the exchange, but we did not own the aircraft we were offering. What we were offering were aircraft that the Navy already owned. We were providing a service of returning the property to its owner. Therefore, Captain Rasmussen's proposition was against the law.

2
Our First Pensacola Contract

Al had an idea: transport them on a 24-foot stake bed truck.

On December 27, 1990, I signed a contract committing A and T Recovery to the locating, recovery, and "delivery of (1) SB2U Aircraft, BuNo 1383 and (1) F4F-3 Aircraft, BuNo 3872 to the National Museum of Naval Aviation, Pensacola, Florida." The contract signing was just after I had delivered the second aircraft, the Grumman F4F-3 Wildcat, Bureau No. 3872, to the museum that we had recovered on December 21. We had already delivered the Vought SB2U-2 Vindicator, 1383, several weeks earlier. In between the recoveries and deliveries, we went to Lake Martin, Alabama, for about a week. There we had located and recovered a missing aircraft that ended the FBI's international manhunt for D. Blan Stewart. All in all, it was a very interesting, exciting, and active few months for us.

We had located both of the Navy's aircraft over two years earlier with relatively little effort. Actually, finding the Vindicator was more of lengthy boat ride than a side-scan sonar search. It was March 20, 1988, the first day of our season out on the lake for that year. Lake Michigan is far enough north that a major percentage of it freezes over in the winter, causing an end to virtually all boating activities, including ours. That day was the first day we felt the ice had receded enough that it was safe to begin operations. To be more exact, the near shore ice was thin enough for us to use our boat to break through. Therefore, we sought to find the Vindicator.

It was a several-hour boat ride to reach the starting point of our search pattern. Not only was it a good distance from shore, but we had to travel up the Chicago River and through the controlling locks. That early in the year, the Chicago Harbor system is closed to boat moorings and our boat was moored at a marine storage facility downriver. We arrived at our starting point, placed the sonar's transponder array in the water, and began our survey with the first line in an easterly direction. On the boat that day were Al, Scott, and I.

We have an unusual set of dynamics and rules among the team of A and T Recovery. The first rule is to do or say things that irritates other members of the team, then argue

The recovery of F4F-3 Wildcat, 3872.

The display of F4F-3 Wildcat, 3872, at the National Naval Aviation Museum.

and banter about what you have said or done for great lengths of time, and finally end the conversation with one of four phrases, "it is your fault," "it is my fault," "it really does not matter," or "no one really cares." That day being the first day of the season started with some such a conversation between Al and me. Scott has long been hard of hearing so his participation was always minimal.

It was not long before we realized that our conversation had distracted us enough to where we had neglected the navigation system and had drifted off course from the survey line. As Al was preparing to correct the issue, an image of an aircraft appeared at the extreme end of the sonar's recording paper on the southern facing channel. Normally, what we would have done was circle back, place the boat in its proper positioning, and re-survey the line. We decide to continue in the same direction then just begin the next survey line to the south, heading in a westerly direction. It was not long until we had a solid image of the Vindicator on the sonar printout. We would not have any such luck with the recovery of the aircraft.

The U.S. Navy's World War II carrier aircraft were designed to use lifting assemblies so that they could be lifted on and off the ships, quickly removed in the event of mishap on the deck, and/or suspended for repairs, maintenance, or other reasons. Instructions on the use of the systems are found in the aircraft "Erection and Maintenance Manuals." Al always liked to use the word "cryptic" when referring to the drawings and explanations of the lifting assemblies found in the manuals. Actually, he used the phrase for everything that is found in those manuals. The instructions for the lifting assembly for a SB2U had a drawing of a wire harness that attached at four points, two forward and two behind the pilot's cockpit—it was for sure cryptic. To be fair, the manual was written and intended to support the training course for the people that would have used the system to handle the aircraft. The lifting assembly was not the only challenge we would have concerning the recovery of the aircraft. She was resting on the lake floor in approximately 160 feet of water, standing on her main landing gear and propeller. The aircraft was in a 45-degree nose down attitude, which added to the complexity of lifting her.

When the time came to recover her, we found the lifting harness stowed and attached at the two points behind the cockpit. The forward attachment fittings were present and the harness appeared to be in very good condition. The forward attachment fittings were "horse shoe"-shaped pieces of stainless steel, with holes for bolts or pins, though the bolt or pin fasteners were missing. From the maintenance manual, we really could not tell where and what the forward fittings attached to, so our first task was to determine what those fittings would be and the type and size of the bolt or pin that was needed. To give a perspective of the difficulty of working underwater in a marine environment, a person on land attaching the lifting harness with the correct size pins would have taken about a minute. After several weeks, we had the harness in place and we were ready to lift.

For many of the World War II aircraft, it was common to have a component made from magnesium as part of the assembly that attached the engine to the air frame—the Vought Vindicator was one of those aircraft. An aircraft on the bottom of Lake Michigan causes a phenomenon to occur called "electrolysis." Over the many years that the aircraft rest on the lake's floor, the magnesium components become the "anode slaves," thus corroding at an accelerated rate. From our visual inspections, the Vindicator appeared completely intact; however, the engine mounting components were hidden from view behind the cowling and other panels. As we began the lift, the aircraft leveled. The Twin Wasp Junior engine, along with the propeller and cowling, detached from the airframe, drastically changing the aircraft's weight and balance. The empennage dropped, putting a strain on the lifting harness in a vector/direction it was not designed, and the apparatus sheared. It was all my fault.

As with all things involving A and T Recovery, we figured out an acceptable method to solve the problems of lifting the newly configured aircraft. On the evening of October 31, 1990, we recovered the last known remaining SB2U-2 Vought Vindicator, 1383, from the depths of Lake Michigan.

I had not bothered to arrange for the shipping of the aircraft because Al had presented the idea of using a 24-foot stake bed truck. It was one of those things we just had to let him try. We rented a truck, loaded the disassembled SB2U aboard, and delivered her late in the afternoon on November 3, 1990. The look on Captain Rasmussen's face was well worth the effort—it was "priceless." He must have thought we had brought him nothing but a truck load of scrap aluminum. After about an hour and half, we had unloaded and placed all the components of the aircraft on the ground in their proper relationship to each other to reveal a true treasure of the Navy's historic aircraft collection.

In exchange for our efforts, we received a number of aircraft engines in storage containers, a Grumman Albatross, and the ownership of several aircraft that were still on the bottom of Lake Michigan. We termed the later trade items as "wet titles." As expeditiously as possible, we removed the aircraft engines and Albatross from the Navy's possession and recovered the wet title aircraft. We turned all of the items over to Mark Clark of Courtesy Aircraft for sale.

The late night lift of Vought SB2U-2 Vindicator, 1383. For some reason, we decided to lift this aircraft as soon as we brought it into the dock. The odd coloration of the aircraft is as a result of the industrial lighting we were using. Although the lights provided us with good visibility, they were the wrong color temperature for photographic work.

Above: Everyone of A and T Recovery's crew at one time sat in the cockpit of one of the recovered aircraft. This happened to be one of those times for John Trojan. In August 2002, John Trojan passed away as a result of complications from multiple myeloma.

Right: The loading of the SB2U-2 into the stake bed truck.

The restored Vought SB2U-2 Vindicator, 1383, now displayed at the National Naval Aviation Museum.

The SBD Dauntless A and T Recovery received in exchange under the conditions of our first contract with the National Museum of Naval Aviation. In the exchange, we also received two Wildcat Fighters. The three aircraft A and T Recovery received in the exchange were purchased by civilian collectors. All three aircraft have been restored to flight capable condition.

3

Who Was D. Blan Stewart?

Boy I knew you were lying.
A local Sheriff

On June 15, 1990, an associate of ours read an article in the *Wall Street Journal* titled "Is Blan Stewart Dead, This Time? A Town Debates the Mystery." The article went into great detail explaining an extraordinary case of an Alabama insurance broker, Blan Stewart, who had gone missing. The author used the term "bizarre" for many reasons: one being that Mr. Stewart's bookkeeper had received a telephone call saying he had died in a plane crash five months before he actually might have died in such a manner. However, people from the FBI, Alabama State prosecutors, several insurance companies, and Alabama Court system seemed to believe he had not died and was very much alive and on the lam. They all seemed to want to argue that Mr. Stewart had somehow faked a plane crash, perhaps by flying a small aircraft over a lake and throwing out aircraft parts for someone to later find. On the line for the interested parties were criminal indictments, the welfare of a spouse and young offspring, and somewhere near $4 million in life insurance. Everything would be determined if it could be proven or disproven that Mr. Stewart was at the bottom of the Lake Martin reservoir, which was formed by the 1923 to 1926 construction of the Martin Dam on the Tallapoosa River, Southern Alabama. The lake is where aircraft debris had been located the morning after Halloween night 1988. It was the perfect story to pique our interest.

After reading the article, Al contacted the family of Mr. Stewart who at the time was represented by Blan's father-in-law, a well-known prestigious Alabama attorney. Our attorney and Mr. Stewart's father-in-law worked out a contract where if we found the aircraft, with Mr. Stewart's remains present, we would receive a percentage of the life insurance policies. If Mr. Stewart's remains were not present, we could attempt to collect on the $100,000 reward that was being offered by one of the insurance companies that Mr. Stewart had conducted business with over the years. The reward was offered for information to his whereabouts. If we were not able to locate the aircraft, we received nothing. We call this sort of contract "No cure. No pay."

After the contract was secured, we set our efforts on finding the aircraft. Al went to the lake to make some drift tests in order for us to determine the most probable location of the aircraft. I located all the possible available data from the National Transportation Safety Board. That information solidified our belief that the aircraft Mr. Stewart had been flying in on that Halloween evening would in fact be at the bottom of the lake. If Mr. Stewart was not with the aircraft, he had to be an unbelievable genius and know a great deal about aircraft accidents in order to fake one that well.

The rented aircraft Mr. Stewart had been flying was a Piper PA-28-181, an Archer II. It is a small four-seat, low-wing, single-engined aircraft with a carburetor. As we understood, Blan had rented the aircraft to fly himself back to Huntsville, Alabama. His intention had been to take his ten-year-old daughter "trick or treating" that evening. He had been in Florida conducting some business. It was close to 6 p.m. as he was nearing Lake Martin when the aircraft began developing engine problems. He notified the Federal Aviation Administration's air traffic control by radio of his situation. They vectored him to the nearest airport, a place to which he did not arrive. We believed that what brought down the aircraft was "carburetor icing"—ice forming in and around the aircraft's carburetor—which is caused when there is a high percentage of moisture in the atmosphere and a low temperature. The conditions that evening were almost perfect for that problem to develop. It should be noted that the aircraft is equipped with a "switch" that allows the pilot to correct the problem. I believe Mr. Stewart may have had multiple issues on his mind and had simply neglected to "flip" that switch.

On Sunday, November 11, 1990, we arrived at Lake Martin ready to begin searching Monday morning. After three days, we had located the aircraft, with Mr. Stewart's remains inside, in 65 feet of water, standing nose down on top of some downed trees. On Friday morning, Al made a call to the family and informed them of our progress.

Mr. Stewart had been under criminal indictment, which stemmed from a claim that he had stolen or defrauded insurance clients out of close to $600,000. I never did find out if that was true, but it sure seemed to bring a lot of attention to the case, which was good for us. During that time period, there was a television program, *America's Most Wanted*, which aired for about twenty-five years, starting in 1988. The episodes highlighted fugitives, and it seemed to be mostly very violent individuals who were being sought by the FBI. The host of the show would ask the audience to call a number if they had any knowledge of the whereabouts of the people who were featured. It was apparently very successful, with over 1,000 criminals being caught as a result of the program. They had produced an episode on Blan Stewart that was to be broadcast nationally on Fox TV on the evening of Friday, November 16, 1990. It was the same day we had made it known that we located the aircraft. That afternoon, Fox TV flew in the program's host, chartered a helicopter to follow our recovery progress, and broadcast live from the lift area. The following week, the host of the TV show delivered a very respectful sincere statement of condolences to the Stewart family.

During our week at Lake Martin, we had located the body of a suicide victim. We learned more than we ever wanted to know about the recovery of drowning victims. We were the "honored" guests at the social event as a result of that discovery. I also had some very awkward interactions with one of the local sheriffs when he attempted to question me about what we were doing on "his" lake. I guess he never did believe my fishing story. To sum it up, we made a lot of money and had an interesting cultural experience for a bunch of guys from the Chicago area. It would not be the last time we would solve a civilian aviation mystery.

The interesting thing about this photograph is that it is taken after the Archer II aircraft, N8211P, reached the lake's surface. We had to tow the aircraft backwards. The backward momentum of the aircraft is seen by the disturbance of the water at the edge of the visible wing and the air lift bags not holding any of the weight of the aircraft.

The beginning of the lift to shore by the crane of Piper PA-28-181, Archer II, N8211P. Mr. Stewart would be identified as the person still in the pilot's seat.

4
We Had to Recover as Many as Possible

Every now and then, even a lawyer has a good idea.

In 1990, the National Museum of Naval Aviation appointed a Deputy Director, "Buddy" Macon. Mr. Macon had a law degree from the Birmingham School of Law. A person with a good understanding of the law would be helpful for the lost aircraft recovery and restoration effort. Soon after he was aboard at the National Museum of Naval Aviation, an idea was conceived to recover and restore as many as possible of the Lake Michigan aircraft. The reason for this was to provide a much greater opportunity for museums, other than the Navy's National Museum of Naval Aviation, to receive aircraft, thereby greatly expanding their presentation to the American public. The Navy's aviation museum is in Pensacola, Florida. It has about 1 million visitors per year, which includes many foreign nationals. Therefore, its visitors are a tiny fraction of the public who are and should be able to see the aircraft. Most museums in the United States struggle economically to keep their doors open. If not for the dedicated volunteers that fill the positions of docents, gift shop attendants, and so many other important roles, few museums in the country would exist. Raising extra money for recovery and restoration of aircraft is very difficult. Understanding this situation, Captain Rasmussen and Buddy Macon set out to ensure that many of the other aviation museums would have the opportunity to receive, on loan, fully restored Wildcat fighters and Dauntless dive-bombers. At the time, there was a considerable amount of valuable Navy exchange assets available for the museum to use to fund such an endeavor. Buddy Macon was tasked with executing what would be a monumental effort in order to rescue as many aircraft as possible.

I remember thinking those are really cool helicopters, but what would we do with them. In order to accomplish the recovery portion of the project, Buddy presented to us a number of flyable, former Army, heavy lift helicopters in exchange for our services. I am sure Al's opinion was exactly the same as mine—everyone would want to have one of those for a toy. However, we needed money, and had to sell the assets in order to recoup our expenditures. We had no way to figure out where on earth to find those people who would want to purchase such an aircraft. It was long before the internet, so we no idea of where to look. That is when the Naval Aviation Museum Foundation joined the effort.

In those days, the Naval Aviation Museum Foundation had a very simple, easy to understand mission and objective: support the National Museum of Naval Aviation. They would raise money to support procurement of aircraft, construction of exhibits, fund janitorial services, the restoration/conservation of aircraft, and many other important efforts that ensured the museum could always keep improving. One of the employees was Captain Ray Hawkins, USN (Ret.). Buddy Macon went to Ray and struck a deal where the foundation would contract with A and T Recovery to locate, recover, and deliver to the Navy a lot of Lake Michigan aircraft. The Navy would transfer the helicopters to the foundation, they would sell them, and then pay A and T Recovery. The idea was simple and it worked when Captain Hawkins and Buddy were able to find a buyer for the helicopters. Since the restoration facilities at the National Museum of Naval Aviation could not handle the large volume of aircraft we were to deliver, Mr. Macon, Captain Hawkins, the Museum, and its foundation had to secure a lot of side restoration exchanges in order to complete the effort.

The recovery of FM-2 Wildcat, 16089, was one of the most entertaining of all of our exploits. We at A and T Recovery really enjoy practical jokes. The closed canopy of this aircraft provided us with a wonderful opportunity. When we recovered the aircraft, people noticed the closed canopy and made the assumption that the pilot must have been trapped inside. Never wanting to disrupt people's morbid fascination with such things, we agreed that it was a possibility. The owner of the boat storage facility where we conducted the lift was the most disturbed. He became completely enraged by the utter lack of concern for the human remains by the crewmembers of A and T Recovery.

The facts of the closed canopy were very simple. When we located the aircraft, she was resting inverted in 234 feet of water. The inverted position was very common for Wildcat Fighters. For some reason, no matter what attitude they would enter the water, they almost always seemed to reach the bottom inverted. What had occurred was that just after crashing, the pilot exited the aircraft unharmed. During his exit, he slid the canopy back part way, failing to engage the latching mechanism. Upon the aircraft's impact with the lake's floor the canopy slammed forward and became latched in a closed position.

Above: National Museum of the Marine Corps (NMMC) restoration staff working on SBD-3 Dauntless, 06583. To ensure that the aircraft could be safely suspended, the NMMC Restoration team spent more than six years and 60,000 man-hours to break the aircraft down completely and then rebuild it. Badly corroded structural pieces were replaced, but as much as possible of the original airframe was retained. Issues with the NMMC's restoration facility aboard Marine Corps Base Quantico had put a temporary halt to the final reassembly and painting of the aircraft. Thankfully, the Smithsonian Institution's National Air & Space Museum graciously provided space at its Steven F. Udvar-Hazy Center to complete the work. This aircraft had been recovered by A and T Recovery on September 13, 1991. (*Photograph courtesy of the National Museum of the Marine Corps*)

Below: Prior to being suspended in the NMMC's central Leatherneck Gallery, the aircraft passed a full load test. This was the first sustained "flight" that 06583 completed since being lost in Lake Michigan in 1943! (*Photograph courtesy of the National Museum of the Marine Corps*)

Painted in the colors of then Major Richard C. Mangrum's "MB-21," the NMMC's SBD-3 is now in place among the other iconic Marine Corps aircraft displayed in Leatherneck Gallery. Major Mangrum was the commanding officer of VMSB-232, which landed at Henderson Field on August 20, 1942 as the first elements of what would become the "Cactus Air Force," and he received the Navy Cross for his attack on the Japanese transport Boston Maru on August 25, 1942. (*Photograph courtesy of the National Museum of the Marine Corps*)

Buddy Macon came up with the idea for a mock underwater exhibit displaying the aircraft as they were found on the lake's floor. This Wildcat is one of the two aircraft placed in the exhibit. That exhibit is very popular at the National Naval Aviation Museum. (*Photograph courtesy of Donald Watson.*)

The beginning of the lift of SBD-4 Dauntless, 06900. Over the years, the Chicago River has been known for being very dirty. This photograph provides a bit of a demonstration of why many people would have that impression.

This Dauntless was recovered from 115 feet deep. The canopy of the aircraft is missing. It appears there must be enough current flow in the lake that over the years the canopy sections became dislodged and were moved away from the aircraft.

Aircraft have to be lifted slowly. One of the longest waits is spent watching water drain from the wings, which is what A and T Recovery crewmembers are doing in this photograph.

SBD-4 Dauntless, 06900, fully out of the water. This aircraft as sent to the San Diego Air & Space Museum.

Al Olson and Taras Lyssenko in their younger years, completely following the U.S. Government's Occupational Safety and Health Administration standards and guidelines when using a crane while lifting TBF-1 Avenger, 01747.

TBF-1 Avenger, 01747, fully out of the water. This aircraft can be seen at the Deland Naval Air Station Museum.

Above left: TBF-1, 01747, had this hand-painted "squadron" emblem on both sides of the aircraft forward of the cockpit. We have never been able to associate it with any actual U.S. Navy squadron. It may have been unauthorized art.

Above right and below: This Wildcat demonstrates what was very common for this type of aircraft. There was a magnesium component that was part of the assembly that attached the engine to the airframe. That part acted as an "anode slave" during all the years underwater. It corroded allowing the engine to become dislodged during the lift.

FM-2 Wildcat, 16089, at the beginning of the lift from water. Note the impact damage to the starboard side of the aircraft.

Note the canopy is closed.

As if it were stenciled on the day before "Navy 16089" still on the vertical stabilizer.

The canopy was clearly closed and latched. The canopy was in this position when we lifted the aircraft.

For some reason, the armaments were present on many of the aircraft used for the carrier qualification as this photograph demonstrates.

This wildcat was located in 240 feet of water. Note the very good condition she was in when recovered.

5
The Early Holocene Forest

Leave it to a Navy pilot to crash in the trees.
Keith Pearson

When you are always doing things people think are a bit crazy, people start to think you are crazy. Even if they know for sure that the things that you tell them you have done in the past are completely true, they tend not to believe you when you tell them something new. This held true with the story of the "Early Holocene Forest," or what the coastal geologists from Northeastern Illinois University named the "Olson Site" in honor of Al. The story that was so hard to believe is that we discovered a previously unknown, over 8,000-year-old forest in the Midwest. Most people might think that almost every forest is over 8,000 years old, not the individual trees but the growth in the area. The enchanted forest we found is located about 15 miles off Chicago, 85 feet deep on the bottom of Lake Michigan, which made it unbelievable. I do not know if there is a cliché that if a story is too unbelievable, do not believe it; however, this one happens to be completely true.

We had located and begun working on a SBD-5 Dauntless, 10575. There was nothing out of the ordinary for us about this aircraft. Nothing that we saw when analyzing and videotaping her posed any difficulty with our recovery effort. However, there were some very odd things surrounding her. To me, they looked similar to super colony anthills. My recollection is that Al and Keith thought they were old wood pilings, but they were randomly distributed on the lake floor. There was no pattern that would indicate being placed there by human beings. As I was very young and flippant at the time, I really did not care what the objects were. Each of them was sticking up through the lakebed sediment. They were about 1–3 feet tall, with a cone shape, and a very dark brown color. Keith really took an interest in them, which resulted in the common Al chastisement that was spoken when a diver underwater was doing something other than working on the aircraft: "No sight-seeing!"

Frank Pranschke, a friend of ours at the time, was a research fellow and limnologist with Northeastern Illinois University. He had one of the most unique talents I have ever seen: he could lick a sample of clay and tell where that clay had originated from thousands of years ago. That talent is very useful for anyon who is studying the movements of glaciers during the ice age. Frank was also the sort of man who could roll his eyes at a person without that person feeling offended. He did just that when Keith tried to explain to him what we had seen. Frank simply smiled, said he was not really interested, and then went back to whatever he was doing at the time. That was not good enough for Keith, who was determined to get Frank's attention. When we returned to the site, Keith broke off several pieces, each a few inches in length, from one of the cones. Upon inspection on the boat, we could all see that the cones were in fact wood, but still did not have any idea why or how they came to be in that location. Keith again returned to bother Frank, this time handing him a piece of the wood. I will never know, because I never asked, if Frank was just humoring Keith, but Frank sent samples to two laboratories for radio-carbon dating. The test results returned data indicating that the wood was 8,300 to 8,100 (RCYBP, whatever that means) years old. Frank Pranschke and his associates at Northeastern Illinois University became very interested.

Frank introduced us to his colleagues Charles Shabica, Ph.D. (Earth Science Professor, Northeastern Illinois University) and Michael Chrzastowski (Coastal Geologist, Illinois State Geologic Survey). The three of them put together a number of grant proposals in order to fund studies of the site. Soon they had the interest of the United States Geologic Survey and the National Geographic Society, because what we had stumbled upon was so unique. The prevailing history of the Great Lakes was that some 12,000 years ago, toward the end of the ice age, glaciers were receding, leaving what we know today as Lake Michigan. The cones we had found were tree stumps, remnants of a forest that had grown at that location some 8,000 years ago. For the geologists, we had located a great treasure because it showed that the conventional understanding of the lake was incorrect. They would have to study the site in great detail in order to correct the historical scientific misunderstandings.

Over the next several years, there would be more side-scan sonar surveys, sub-bottom profile surveys, many substrate core samples taken, and samples of the tree stumps taken and studied to determine their species. There were even lake water current direction and velocity studies. The work involved researchers from a wide spectrum of scientific fields, including anthropology as there was hope of locating evidence of occupation by Paleo-Americans at the site. The efforts showed that the trees, including oak and ash, had once lived on the banks of an ancient river system, a precursor to the Chicago River. This river was there when the Lake Michigan water level was so low that the researchers called it Lake Chippewa. Apparently, there was a fork in the river at the location of the stumps. For some reason, because of that river and the surrounding geography when the waters of Lake Michigan did swell to the size it is in the modern day, sediment surrounded the trees and protected their stumps from decay for over 8,000 years. All this was discovered and learned because a Navy pilot during World War II crashed in the trees.

One of the first photographs taken by Keith Pearson of one of the early Holocene forest tree stumps. The photograph demonstrates that lack of water clarity at the time even at only 85 feet deep.

A and T Recovery diver using an underwater chain saw in order to retrieve a tree stump sample.

Above left: It had to be demonstrated that the stumps were actually attached to roots in order to prove they were trees and not pilings. This photograph was taken to show the depth in the lake's floor where the roots were found.

Above right: Scott Lyssenko holding one of the retrieved stump samples.

Opposite above: One of the rare photographs of Frank Pranschke. In the photograph, he is interacting with Keith Pearson on the back of A and T Recovery's vessel.

Opposite below: Frank Pranschke supervising Allan Olson, Scott Lyssenko, and Taras Lyssenko as they prepare the coring assembly.

6

Trying to do Something Against the Law, Change the Law

Doesn't everyone change the law when it does not work for their needs?

Is it not logical that when the law does not work for what you wish to do that you simply change it? It made perfect sense to us, it is what everyone does when the law does not work. In conversations with Captain Rasmussen that is what seemed to be the only option that would work in order for us to be able to recover the lost Lake Michigan Navy aircraft on behalf of the National Museum of Naval Aviation and receive compensation. If nothing else, we were all in for a civics' learning experience.

The average person in the United States believes it is not an easy task to change federal law, and they are absolutely correct. Being part of the Navy, Captain Rasmussen was not permitted to simply tell the U.S. Congress the language of a bill to fix our issue. Someone other than he had to make such a proposal—fortunately, someone did. The National Museum of Naval Aviation Museum is in the First U.S. Congressional District of Florida. At the time, Earl Dewitt Hutto was that district's representative to the US House of Representatives. Representative Hutto sponsored a bill that would correct our problem.

There was not really much to the legislation, a change of a few words that would add "services" to be allowed in exchanges was all that it requested. Realizing that such a bill would not have a very high priority in the business of the U.S. Congress, Al and I decided we would try our hand at lobbying. Not knowing what we were doing, our plan was to send letters to every member of Congress suggesting they should support the legislation. Al thought the letters should be signed by his father who was a member of one of the many veterans' organizations. In those days, it was not just the click of a keyboard on the computer to send a note to your or any congressional member. We had to do a lot of work to produce 534 letters. One was missing, we did not need to send one to Representative Hutto.

It took some time, but the bill passed both houses of Congress. However, changes in Title 10 U.S. Code § 2572 came with changes in regulation. I guess that can be described as the rules by which the law can be applied. The Navy had to develop the regulations for their museums. They termed the regulation as SECNAVINST 5755.1 (Secretary of the Navy Instruction), Department of the Navy Museum Exchanges. The document was about six pages long, with specific rules to accomplish the exchanges. There were statements that dealt with the types of items the Navy could exchange and what the Navy could receive in return. There was a solid rule that the Navy had to DEMIL (demilitarization) all exchange property. They could transfer books, manuscripts, works of art, historical artifacts, drawings, plans, models, and condemned or obsolete combat materiel, when such assets are no longer needed by the department. The Department of the Navy could accept assets or services that were similar items, conservation supplies, equipment, facilities, or search, salvage, transportation, restoration, conservation, preservation services, or educational programs. We cared about search, salvage, transportation, restoration, conservation, and preservation services. The good thing is that it had become legal for us to recover the aircraft and be compensated.

7
UC-97

Sure, yeah, right, there is a German World War I U-boat on the bottom of Lake Michigan.

It is sort of funny how so often in the shipwreck exploration world the cliché "Holy Grail" is used. The *UC-97* is one of those vessels to which the term has been applied. The ship is for sure not any sort of holy anything, but it does have one of the most interesting stories of any difficult-to-find shipwreck. Al, Scott, a friend of mine Teila, and I located her on July 10, 1992, after four years and about 140 square miles of side-scan sonar searching.

The ship was a UC Type III minelaying submarine of the German Imperial Navy (*Kaiserliche Marine*). She was built in 1917–1918 by Blohm & Voss in Hamburg, Germany. The same company years later would build the mighty *Bismarck* battleship. The *UC-97* was delivered and commissioned shortly before the Great War ended, but she was never placed into wartime service. Late in 1918, she, along with about 170 other *Kaiserliche Marine* submarines, were surrendered to the Allies and the United States of America. She became one of six that were allocated and transferred to the United States.

In 1919, American crews took possession of the six boats and sailed for the United States, calling their fleet the Former German Submarine Expeditionary Force. The boats were commissioned in the U.S. Navy, with the ship's log pages for the *UC-97* calling her the *United States Ship Ex-German Submarine UC-97*. The Expeditionary Force crossed the Atlantic Ocean heading to the Azores, then traveled on to New York Harbor. There, the boats separated, heading off on tours, bond drives, and for study by the U.S. Navy. *UC-97* was sent to tour the Great Lakes, arriving in Chicago during the summer of 1919.

The residents of Chicago were allotted time to view the submarine, which was considered one of the two extreme terror weapons of the Great War—the other weapon being sulfur mustard, commonly known as mustard gas. The sinking of the R.M.S. *Lusitania* by a submarine became a major factor in the U.S.A.'s decision to declare war on Germany. After the war, many Americans wanted to see these horrible weapons up

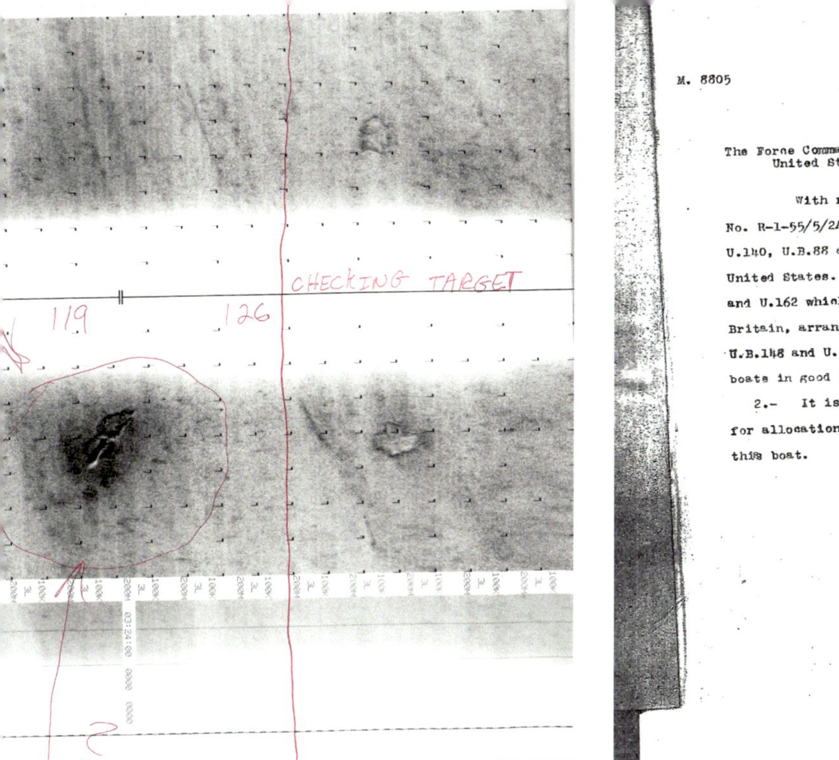

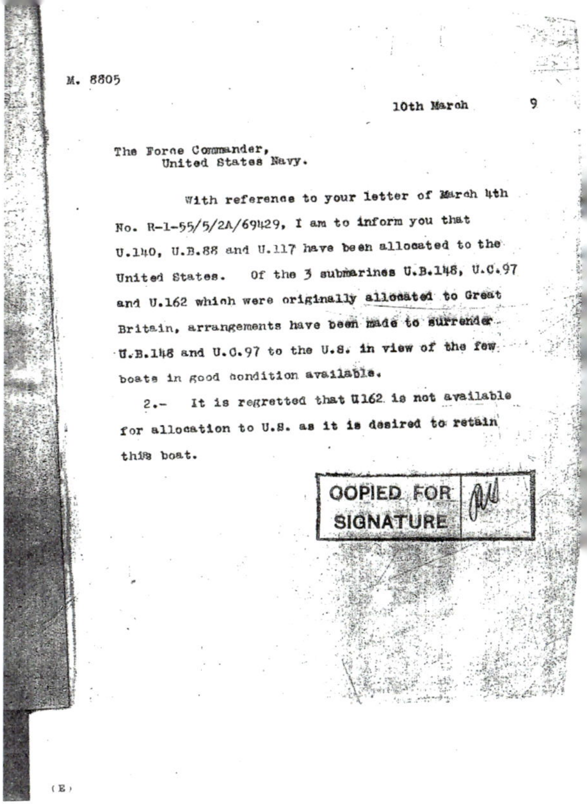

M. 8805

10th March 9

The Force Commander,
United States Navy.

With reference to your letter of March 4th No. R-1-55/5/2A/69429, I am to inform you that U.140, U.B.88 and U.117 have been allocated to the United States. Of the 3 submarines U.B.148, U.C.97 and U.162 which were originally allocated to Great Britain, arrangements have been made to surrender U.B.148 and U.C.97 to the U.S. in view of the few boats in good condition available.

2.- It is regretted that U162 is not available for allocation to U.S. as it is desired to retain this boat.

COPIED FOR SIGNATURE

(E)

Above left: This is the first image of U.S.S. *Ex-German Submarine UC-97* we had on our side-scan sonar printout.

Above right: Correspondence from the British Royal Navy surrendering *UC-97* and other submarines to the U.S. Navy.

Below: Former World War I German submarines *UB-88*, *UB-148*, and *UC-97* moored together. Note the crews appear to have an interest in the deck guns. (*From the collection of Lt. O. E. Wightman of WWI and WWII-era images, the Naval Historical Foundation*)

Wreath ceremony aboard the former German U-boat *UC-97* on the four-year anniversary of the sinking of S.S. *Lusitania*.

Former German World War I German Submarines *UB-88*, *UC-97*, and *U-117* in the Brooklyn Navy Yard, April 29, 1919. (*Courtesy of the Naval History and Heritage Command*)

UC-97 during her visit to Milwaukee. (*Photo courtesy of the Great Lakes Marine Collection of the Milwaukee Public Library/Wisconsin Marine Historical Society*)

close. At the time, it was thought that the world, perhaps the League of Nations, would outlaw the use of submarines in warfare.

After some time of being on public display in Chicago, the Navy set about the task of removing specific components from the U-boat for analysis. At that time, the *Kaiserliche Marine*'s submarines were far superior to those of the U.S. Navy. It had been noted by the *UC-97*'s Great Lakes' tour commander, Charles A. Lockwood, that the German submarines could "dive" a lot faster than those of the Americans. One of the submarine's engines, the periscope, and a lot of other components were removed and sent for study to different bureaus of the Department of the Navy. On June 7, 1921, the U.S. Ship Ex-German Submarine *UC-97* was towed into deep water within the South Basin of Lake Michigan and shelled by the U.S.S. *Wilmette* until she sank.

There was a bit of irony to that vessel sinking the U-boat. The Navy training vessel U.S.S. *Wilmette* had once been the ill-fated S.S. *Eastland*, which had rolled over in the Chicago River on July 24, 1914, causing the greatest maritime disaster in Great Lakes' history. A total of 844 passengers and crew died in that single event.

It was Al who really wanted to find the *UC-97*. He had put a lot of time into studying the logs of the U-boat, the U.S.S. *Hawk*, the ship that had towed the *UC-97* out into the lake on her last voyage, and the U.S.S. *Wilmette*. He put together a dedicated chart of the southern basin of the lake, where he had drawn arcs indicating both the closest and farthest possible distances the vessel could be resting from Chicago's harbor. Al would use colored markers to fill in sections on the chart to indicate that we had completed searching an area. Sometimes the color would be red, green, or blue. For some reason, I thought he was doing some sort of color coding system until the day I asked him why

The wreck of the *Eastland* in the Chicago River, Library of Congress, Kaufmann, Weimer & Fabry Co.

each color. The reason was that happened to be the color marker he found first that day. Our boat is always a bit messy, we constantly misplace pens, pencils, scuba masks, and just about anything smaller than a football.

On the day we located the *UC-97*, an entirely different discovery expedition began. There are people who search for things that are lost to time simply to find them. We do what we do in an attempt to recover and bring those lost wonders back to society. If you recall my story of the wallet being lost in a parking lot, the same theory would apply with the *UC-97* but with a few twists. The ship's apparent owner, to us, had been the U.S. Navy, but they intentionally threw it away—shelling and sinking it. Answering the question of who now owned it was a bit more complex and became our next quest.

We might have said that A and T Recovery now owned it, but a number of people started making claims that they had found it before A and T Recovery. One said that he had been out on the lake using an old World War II sonar searching for the *UC-97*. He had done a number of swaths somewhere out there when he "burned out" a tube and the sonar screen went "elliptical." I took that to mean his search equipment broke. Somehow by his odd logic, he had found the U-boat. Another person claimed that he had made a request of the U.S. Navy to fly a P-3 Orion submarine hunting aircraft over the lake and that the Navy had honored that request. The magnetometer aboard the P-3 indicated there was a chunk of steel in the lake, therefore he was the "official" finder of *UC-97*. There are other big hunks of steel out at the bottom of Lake Michigan, we found several of them.

Actually, the true indictor of who had claim to the vessel came from a federal law passed in 1988. That law, termed the "Abandoned Shipwreck Act," seemed to indicate that *UC-97* would be property of the State of Illinois. That was because the Navy intentionally sank her. We agreed with that legal analysis.

In order to test our belief of who owns the vessel, George Hesik, our attorney at the time, filed a friendly lawsuit against the State of Illinois in the Court of Claims. All possible claimants were notified, which included the U.S. Navy and even the British Royal Navy. People had told me that they felt the German Navy might have some claim. We never agreed with such thinking, especially since *UC-97* was from World War I and Germany had put the world through a second far more devastating war. An idea that the Royal Navy had some claim came from the staff at the Naval Historical Center.

They wanted to assert that since the boat had been originally surrendered to the British Navy, it must still be belong to them. It was flawed logic. The reason the submarines and the surface ships of the German Navy were turned over to the British was that they had geographically close harbors that could handle the surrendered vessels. On April 15, 1996, the Court of Claims made a legal determination that the State of Illinois is in fact the owner of U.S.S. *Ex-German Submarine UC-97*.

If we had been able to raise the needed funds to recover and restore the sub, A and T Recovery's part in this story might have ended soon after that legal determination, but we could only have been so lucky. At the time we located *UC-97*, interest in the vessel was strong, but quickly fell off and would not appear again for another twenty years. In 2016, there was a chance that a very wealthy person had an interest in the recovery. I notified the vessel's owner and also the Naval History and Heritage Command (the name for the former Naval Historical Center). No matter the ownership of the vessel, it is still an exciting part of U.S. Naval history, and they should be involved. What was I thinking, I must enjoy dealing with utter insanity. Some of the same staff that had been there in the 1990s were still there in 2016. Again they brought forth the notion that *UC-97* was owned by the Royal Navy. However, this time they went to the International Law Division of the U.S. Navy, gave them a handful of documents, and asked for their legal opinion. For sure that must be the way to achieve a correct legal opinion, tell a fraction of the story. The staff at the Naval History and Heritage Command received the opinion they sought. The International Law Division felt that *UC-97* was the property of the Royal Navy.

For months, I was told that the Naval History and Heritage Command was intending to draft and send a letter to the Royal Navy requesting their legal opinion. The legal counsel of the Naval History and Heritage Command kept claiming it would be beneficial for A and T Recovery if the Royal Navy owned the vessel. The Naval History and Heritage Command never sent the letter, and I do not believe one was ever drafted. I sent a letter to the First Sea Lord of the Royal Navy, and the response I received was plain and simple: "... we consider that ownership of *UC-97* was transferred to US authorities post-WWI..."

This was one of the many times that the staff of the Naval Historical Center/Navy History and Heritage Command would attempt to thwart our efforts. We are still working on securing funding for the recovery, restoration, and display of *UC-97*. I believe if we are successful, the staff at the Naval History and Heritage Command will again do their best to attempt to undermine our efforts.

Commodore Martin Connell Royal Navy

British Naval Attaché
British Embassy
3100 Massachusetts Ave, NW
Washington, DC
United States

Telephone: 202 588 6802
Facsimile: 202 588 7871
Email: BDSUS-RN-NA@mod.uk

Mr Taras C. Lyssenko
A and T Recovery
26351 Hospital Street
Cassopolis
Michigan 49031

13 June 2017

Dear Mr Lyssenko,

Thank you for recently forwarding to me a copy of your letter of 3 January 2017 sent to Admiral Sir Philip Jones regarding the former World War I submarine UC-97. Admiral Jones was grateful for the background information on your proposed project, and he has asked me to respond to you on his behalf. I have now had the opportunity to discuss the matter with the relevant UK authorities. While the Royal Navy is certainly interested in the historical aspects of your proposed project, we consider that ownership of UC-97 was transferred to US authorities post-WWI on the basis that it was used for set purposes and then destroyed or sunk, which is what appears to have happened. We are not aware of any provision made within such agreement for any subsequent remains to be the responsibility of the UK. I have recently written to the Director of the Naval History and Heritage Command to advise him of this decision.

In the meantime we wish you well with your proposed recovery project. We both share the same desire to preserve such historically important submarines for future generations and I hope you are able to successfully recover it intact from Lake Michigan.

Yours sincerely,

The Royal Navy's response to Taras Lyssenko's letter to Admiral Sir Philip Jones about ownership of *UC-97*.

8

The Naval Historical Center Had Become Involved

If there is one thing people in Washington are good at, it is attempting to mess up a project.

Throughout 1991–1993, things were going along quite nicely. As with all things in life, there is always someone out there who believes they can do a better job or that they should be in charge of what others do well. It is especially true with the branch of the U.S. Navy that in the 1990s was called the Naval Historical Center. Today, they are called the Naval History and Heritage Command. The word "Command" creates an oxymoron for it has been clearly evident that their primary purpose, at least with a good number of their staff at the upper management level, is to obstruct. The people at the lower levels that archive documents, photographs, and answer requests for information from the public are dedicated, qualified, and responsive government employees.

I guess if you view the world from the point of view of the upper management of the Naval Historical Center, some understanding of their behavior might be achieved. A good number of them spent years in college studying history, archeology, or some related field only to obtain a job where they review, perhaps document, and criticize the actions of others. Their domains are tiny cubicles where they toil over menial tasks while attempting to justify their existence to themselves and others. They try to overcome the mundaneness of their everyday existence by going to conferences where they and other similar individuals walk around calling each other doctor. They present lackluster papers they have written to sleeping fifteen-person audiences of other boring people.

In the infinite wisdom of the upper command of the U.S. Navy, the National Museum of Naval Aviation was placed under the direction of Naval Historical Center. With almost every bureaucracy in the United States of America, the unspoken rule is that if they are put in charge, in any manner, of a successful program, they must do everything they can to mess it up. In the case of our Lake Michigan once-lost World War II Navy aircraft recovery effort, they fell over themselves attempting to do a good job.

We, Al and I, first became aware of them when Captain Rasmussen and Buddy Macon explained the Center had brought on some former archeologist from the State of Wisconsin.

That person's task was to develop the reporting template (my paraphrase) that was to be used when seeking approval for a recovery of an aircraft. Aircraft recovery was therefore to be halted until that template was drafted. As I recall, about six months later, we were told that the document was ready. What we were presented with would have taken me or anyone else with three functioning brain cells about an hour to prepare.

Later, in 2018, as a result of Freedom of Information Act, requests submitted to the Naval History and Heritage Command and the Michigan State Police, we located documents that showed what that archeologist and other staff of the Naval Historical Center were really actively pursuing. They were conducting a defamation campaign against the staff at the National Museum of Naval Aviation, the Naval Aviation Museum Foundation, and A and T Recovery. The intent of their efforts was to halt the recovery of the Lake Michigan aircraft. The archeologist and other staff at Naval Historical Center maliciously triggered investigations by the FBI, Naval Criminal Investigative Service, the Army Corps of Engineers, and the Michigan State Police all in an attempt to take full control of the lost Lake Michigan aircraft recovery effort. They used rumor, innuendo, distortion of fact, and even flat out lies in attempts to thwart our efforts and end the project. After conducting their research, the investigating parties all saw the actions of the Naval Historical Center's staff for what they really were. The defining incident came when the FBI was telephoned by an anonymous party claiming that A and T Recovery was in the process of stealing a Navy aircraft. Five well-armed FBI agents responded by surrounding Al and me. One telephone call to Captain Rasmussen was all the FBI agents needed for them to gain the understanding that the staff at the Naval Historical Center were really the people who were harming the interests of the people of the United States of America.

Historic Aircraft Wreck Report
Naval Historical Center

Please print or type information in spaces provided. Attach additional sheets if necessary. If not applicable enter "N/A."

Aircraft model: Serial/bureau numbers:
Manufacturer:
Age of aircraft (dates of construction and loss) Built: Lost:
Precise wreck location (lat/long in degrees, minutes, and seconds):
Body of water (name of lake, bay, river, strait, ocean):
Government jurisdiction (name of state, territory, province, or nation, none if in international waters):

Closest land, island, or town:
Depth of water over wrecksite:
Wreck condition (intact, broken, scattered, etc.):

Observable damage (combat damage, missing or altered components):

Probable cause(s) of crash (ditched, combat loss, out of fuel, fire, explosion, high-speed impact, etc.)

Specific observations (canopy, escape hatches, personal access doors open or closed; landing gear extended or retracted; flap positions; instrument and control condition, etc.):

Crash narrative (brief description of crash, based on historical records or oral accounts):

	Yes	No	Comments
Weapons, pyrotechnics, ordnance, or other explosives (ejection seats, cable cutters) present?	☐	☐	
Human remains present?	☐	☐	
Fragile equipment aboard (gunsights, bombsights, gun camera or photo-reconnaissance cameras, film, radios, radar units, other instruments, optical, photographic, and electronic equipment)?	☐	☐	
Other artifacts present (including mapcases, documents, clothing, sidearms, survival, rescue, navigation, or personal equipment)?	☐	☐	

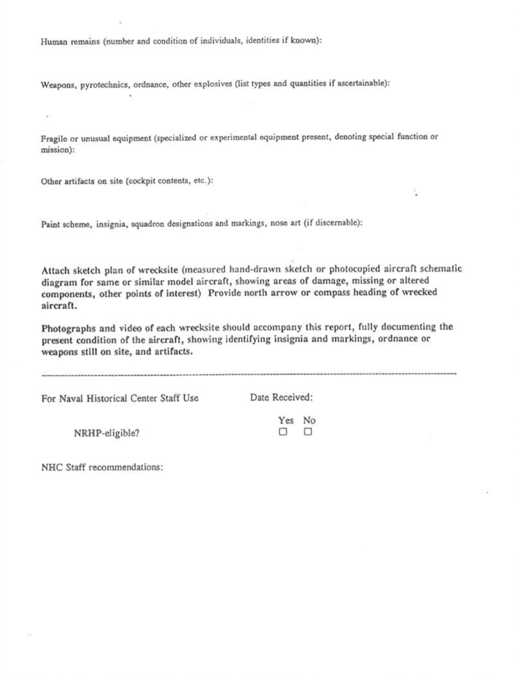

Human remains (number and condition of individuals, identities if known):

Weapons, pyrotechnics, ordnance, other explosives (list types and quantities if ascertainable):

Fragile or unusual equipment (specialized or experimental equipment present, denoting special function or mission):

Other artifacts on site (cockpit contents, etc.):

Paint scheme, insignia, squadron designations and markings, nose art (if discernable):

Attach sketch plan of wrecksite (measured hand-drawn sketch or photocopied aircraft schematic diagram for same or similar model aircraft, showing areas of damage, missing or altered components, other points of interest) Provide north arrow or compass heading of wrecked aircraft.

Photographs and video of each wrecksite should accompany this report, fully documenting the present condition of the aircraft, showing identifying insignia and markings, ordnance or weapons still on site, and artifacts.

For Naval Historical Center Staff Use Date Received:

	Yes	No
NRHP-eligible?	☐	☐

NHC Staff recommendations:

The grand product of months of effort of the great underwater archeologist.

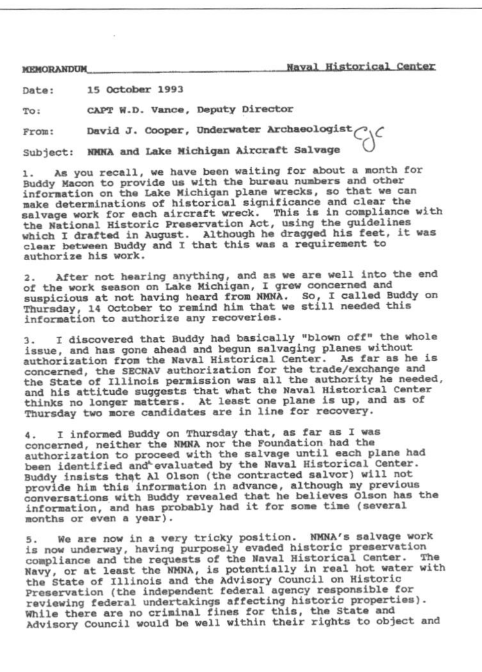

MEMORANDUM Naval Historical Center

Date: 15 October 1993

To: CAPT W.D. Vance, Deputy Director

From: David J. Cooper, Underwater Archaeologist

Subject: NMNA and Lake Michigan Aircraft Salvage

1. As you recall, we have been waiting for about a month for Buddy Macon to provide us with the bureau numbers and other information on the Lake Michigan plane wrecks, so that we can make determinations of historical significance and clear the salvage work for each aircraft wreck. This is in compliance with the National Historic Preservation Act, using the guidelines which I drafted in August. Although he dragged his feet, it was clear between Buddy and I that this was a requirement to authorize his work.

2. After not hearing anything, and as we are well into the end of the work season on Lake Michigan, I grew concerned and suspicious at not having heard from NMNA. So, I called Buddy on Thursday, 14 October to remind him that we still needed this information to authorize any recoveries.

3. I discovered that Buddy had basically "blown off" the whole issue, and has gone ahead and begun salvaging planes without authorization from the Naval Historical Center. As far as he is concerned, the SECNAV authorization for the trade/exchange and the State of Illinois permission was all the authority he needed, and his attitude suggests that what the Naval Historical Center thinks no longer matters. At least one plane is up, and as of Thursday two more candidates are in line for recovery.

4. I informed Buddy on Thursday that, as far as I was concerned, neither the NMNA nor the Foundation had the authorization to proceed with the salvage until each plane had been identified and evaluated by the Naval Historical Center. Buddy insists that Al Olson (the contracted salvor) will not provide him this information in advance, although my previous conversations with Buddy revealed that he believes Olson has the information, and has probably had it for some time (several months or even a year).

5. We are now in a very tricky position. NMNA's salvage work is now underway, having purposely evaded historic preservation compliance and the requests of the Naval Historical Center. The Navy, or at least the NMNA, is potentially in real hot water with the State of Illinois and the Advisory Council on Historic Preservation (the independent federal agency responsible for reviewing federal undertakings affecting historic properties). While there are no criminal fines for this, the State and Advisory Council would be well within their rights to object and

2

stop the salvage work. In some past cases against federal agencies (including the Navy), civil litigation has also resulted, with work delays and forfeitures (these are essentially civil, rather than criminal, fines). The Naval Historical Center could also conceivably instigate law enforcement activities against the salvor or the Naval Aviation Foundation for unauthorized recovery of federal property.

6. I have informed Dr. Dudley, CU, and AVH branches about this, but have no authority myself to stop the work. I have made it clear to Macon that he does not have the authorization to proceed with salvage, at least as far as I am concerned.

7. At your first opportunity, Dr. Dudley and I would like to meet with you to discuss the best way to handle this situation.

Above and below: Some of the many reports by investigators looking into the claims of the staff of the Naval Historical Center.

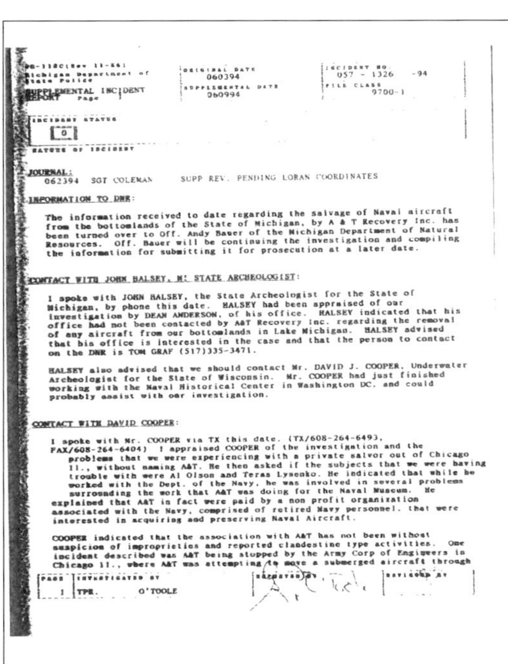

Michigan Department of State Police
SUPPLEMENTAL INCIDENT REPORT Page 1

ORIGINAL DATE 060394
SUPPLEMENTAL DATE 060994
INCIDENT NO. 057 - 1326 -94
FILE CLASS 9700-1

INCIDENT STATUS 0

NATURE OF INCIDENT

JOURNAL:
062394 SGT COLEMAN SUPP REV. PENDING LORAN COORDINATES

INFORMATION TO DNR:

The information received to date regarding the salvage of Naval aircraft from the bottomlands of the State of Michigan, by A & T Recovery Inc. has been turned over to Off. Andy Bauer of the Michigan Department of Natural Resources. Off. Bauer will be continuing the investigation and compiling the information for submitting it for prosecution at a later date.

CONTACT WITH JOHN HALSEY, MI STATE ARCHEOLOGIST:

I spoke with JOHN HALSEY, the State Archeologist for the State of Michigan, by phone this date. HALSEY had been appraised of our investigation by DEAN ANDERSON, of his office. HALSEY indicated that his office had not been contacted by A&T Recovery Inc. regarding the removal of any aircraft from our bottomlands in Lake Michigan. HALSEY advised that his office is interested in the case and that the person to contact on the DNR is TOM GRAF (517)335-3471.

HALSEY also advised that we should contact Mr. DAVID J. COOPER, Underwater Archeologist for the State of Wisconsin. Mr. COOPER had just finished working with the Naval Historical Center in Washington DC. and could probably assist with our investigation.

CONTACT WITH DAVID COOPER:

I spoke with Mr. COOPER via TX this date. (TX/608-264-6493, FAX/608-264-6404) I appraised COOPER of the investigation and the problems that we were experiencing with a private salvor out of Chicago Il., without naming A&T. He then asked if the subjects that we were having trouble with were Al Olson and Teras Lysenko. He indicated that while he worked with the Dept. of the Navy, he was involved in several problems surrounding the work that A&T was doing for the Naval Museum. He explained that A&T in fact were paid by a non profit organization associated with the Navy, comprised of retired Navy personnel, that were interested in acquiring and preserving Naval Aircraft.

COOPER indicated that the association with A&T has not been without suspicion of improprieties and reported clandestine type activities. One incident described was A&T being stopped by the Army Corp of Engineers in Chicago Il., where A&T was attempting to move a submerged aircraft through

PAGE 1 INVESTIGATED BY TPR. O'TOOLE APPROVED BY REVIEWED BY

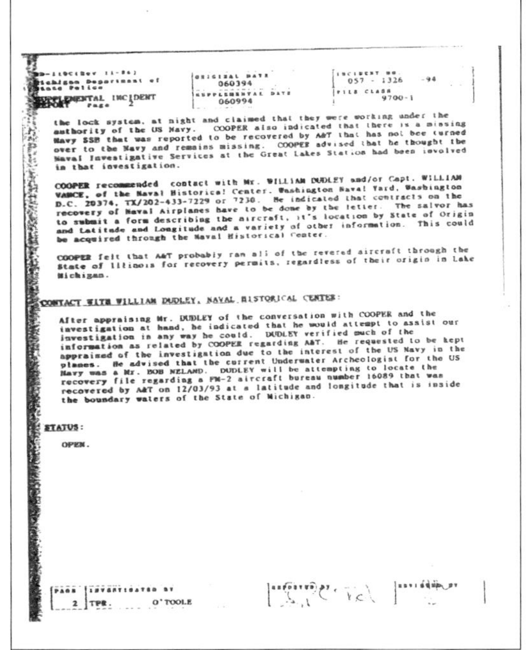

Michigan Department of State Police
SUPPLEMENTAL INCIDENT REPORT Page 2

ORIGINAL DATE 060394
SUPPLEMENTAL DATE 060994
INCIDENT NO. 057 - 1326 -94
FILE CLASS 9700-1

the lock system, at night and claimed that they were working under the authority of the US Navy. COOPER also indicated that there is a missing Navy SSB that was reported to be recovered by A&T that has not bee turned over to the Navy and remains missing. COOPER advised that he thought the Naval Investigative Services at the Great Lakes Station had been involved in that investigation.

COOPER recommended contact with Mr. WILLIAM DUDLEY and/or Capt. WILLIAM VANCE, of the Naval Historical Center, Washington Naval Yard, Washington D.C. 20374, TX/202-433-7229 or 7230. He indicated that contracts on the recovery of Naval Airplanes have to be done by the letter. The salvor has to submit a form describing the aircraft, it's location by State of Origin and Latitude and Longitude and a variety of other information. This could be acquired through the Naval Historical Center.

COOPER felt that A&T probably ran all of the revered aircraft through the State of Illinois for recovery permits, regardless of their origin in Lake Michigan.

CONTACT WITH WILLIAM DUDLEY, NAVAL HISTORICAL CENTER:

After appraising Mr. DUDLEY of the conversation with COOPER and the investigation at hand, he indicated that he would attempt to assist our investigation in any way he could. DUDLEY verified much of the information as related by COOPER regarding A&T. He requested to be kept appraised of the investigation due to the interest of the US Navy in the planes. He advised that the current Underwater Archeologist for the US Navy was a Mr. BOB NELAND. DUDLEY will be attempting to locate the recovery file regarding a FM-2 aircraft bureau number 16089 that was recovered by A&T on 12/03/93 at a latitude and longitude that is inside the boundary waters of the State of Michigan.

STATUS:

OPEN.

PAGE 2 INVESTIGATED BY TPR. O'TOOLE APPROVED BY REVIEWED BY

9

And Then There Was "Midway Madness"

She sure has a lot of bullet holes.

Of all the aircraft the Navy lost in Lake Michigan, the most significant one is SBD-2 Dauntless, 2106. This aircraft is arguably the most important artifact in the Navy's entire historic collection. She was both a veteran of the Japanese Imperial Navy's attack on Pearl Harbor and the Battle of Midway. During the Battle of Midway, her pilot, 1Lt. Daniel Iverson, U.S. Marine Corps, and radioman-gunner, Private First Class Wallace Reid, flew the dive-bomber against the overwhelming Imperial Japanese armada. During the engagement, the Dauntless would receive scores of hits from anti-aircraft gunfire, but would still bring her crew safely home. She was given the nickname *Midway Madness*.

When the time came to recover this aircraft, the Naval Historical Center's archeologist really outdid himself. His first demand before the Naval Historical Center would approve the recovery of the aircraft was that he would have to be brought out by A and T Recovery to the crash site. Once there, we were to allow him to scuba dive on the aircraft so that he could make his "professional" determination of its viability for recovery. After we were to do that, and once he made his determination, he was then to be brought out when any work was being performed on the aircraft so that he personally could claim that he supervised the recovery. It was the position of the Naval Historical Center's person that if his demands were not met, the aircraft would never be recovered. He was willing to keep a national treasure from the American public to feed his ego. He did not care that there was no way that we could allow him to do what he was demanding for it was against OSHA and Navy regulations. Those regulations would not allow us to let him scuba dive from our vessel to the depth of the aircraft. Additionally, our insurance would not provide coverage for him if we did allow such an activity, putting us in legal and financial jeopardy. Realizing that the person did not have the intellect to recover a toy aircraft from his own bath tub, Captain Rasmussen and Buddy Macon stood their ground during months of debate over the matter. In the end, the Naval Historical Center's archeologist was not allowed anywhere near the

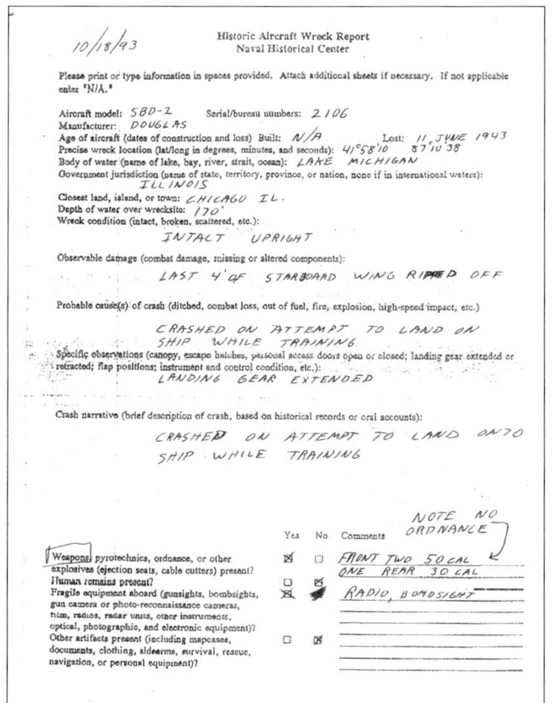

10/18/93

Historic Aircraft Wreck Report
Naval Historical Center

Please print or type information in spaces provided. Attach additional sheets if necessary. If not applicable enter "N/A."

Aircraft model: SBD-2 Serial/bureau numbers: 2106
Manufacturer: DOUGLAS
Age of aircraft (dates of construction and loss) Built: N/A Lost: 11, JUNE 1943
Precise wreck location (lat/long in degrees, minutes, and seconds): 41°58'10 87°10'38
Body of water (name of lake, bay, river, strait, ocean): LAKE MICHIGAN
Government jurisdiction (name of state, territory, province, or nation, none if in international waters): ILLINOIS
Closest land, island, or town: CHICAGO IL.
Depth of water over wrecksite: 170'
Wreck condition (intact, broken, scattered, etc.): INTACT UPRIGHT

Observable damage (combat damage, missing or altered components): LAST 4' OF STARBOARD WING RIPPED OFF

Probable cause(s) of crash (ditched, combat loss, out of fuel, fire, explosion, high-speed impact, etc.) CRASHED ON ATTEMPT TO LAND ON SHIP WHILE TRAINING.

Specific observations (canopy, escape hatches, personal access doors open or closed; landing gear extended or retracted; flap positions; instrument and control condition, etc.): LANDING GEAR EXTENDED

Crash narrative (brief description of crash, based on historical records or oral accounts): CRASHED ON ATTEMPT TO LAND ONTO SHIP WHILE TRAINING

NOTE NO ORDNANCE

	Yes	No	Comments
Weapons, pyrotechnics, ordnance, or other explosives (ejection seats, cable cutters) present?	☒	☐	FRONT TWO 50 CAL ONE REAR 30 CAL
Human remains present?	☐	☒	
Fragile equipment aboard (gunsights, bombsights, gun camera or photo-reconnaissance cameras, film, radios, radar units, other instruments, optical, photographic, and electronic equipment)?	☒	■	RADIO, BOMBSIGHT
Other artifacts present (including mapcases, documents, clothing, sidearms, survival, rescue, navigation, or personal equipment)?	☐	☒	

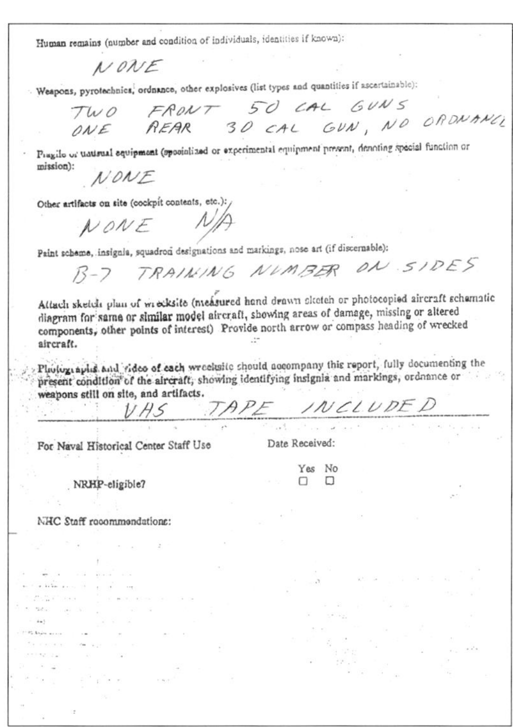

Human remains (number and condition of individuals, identities if known): NONE

Weapons, pyrotechnics, ordnance, other explosives (list types and quantities if ascertainable): TWO FRONT 50 CAL GUNS ONE REAR 30 CAL GUN, NO ORDNANCE

Fragile or unusual equipment (specialized or experimental equipment present, denoting special function or mission): NONE

Other artifacts on site (cockpit contents, etc.): NONE N/A

Paint scheme, insignia, squadron designations and markings, nose art (if discernable): B-7 TRAINING NUMBER ON SIDES

Attach sketch plan of wrecksite (measured hand drawn sketch or photocopied aircraft schematic diagram for same or similar model aircraft, showing areas of damage, missing or altered components, other points of interest) Provide north arrow or compass heading of wrecked aircraft.

Photographs and video of each wrecksite should accompany this report, fully documenting the present condition of the aircraft, showing identifying insignia and markings, ordnance or weapons still on site, and artifacts.

VHS TAPE INCLUDED

For Naval Historical Center Staff Use Date Received:

	Yes	No
NRHP-eligible?	☐	☐

NHC Staff recommendations:

Above, below and next two pages: We at A and T Recovery always complied with the demands of the Naval Historical Center as demonstrated by our pre-recovery report of "Midway Madness."

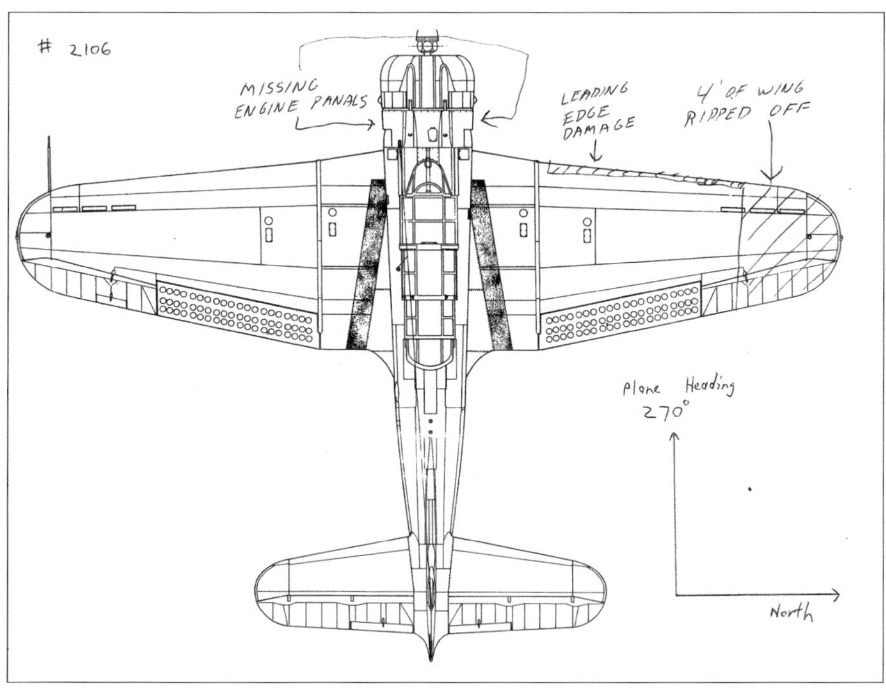

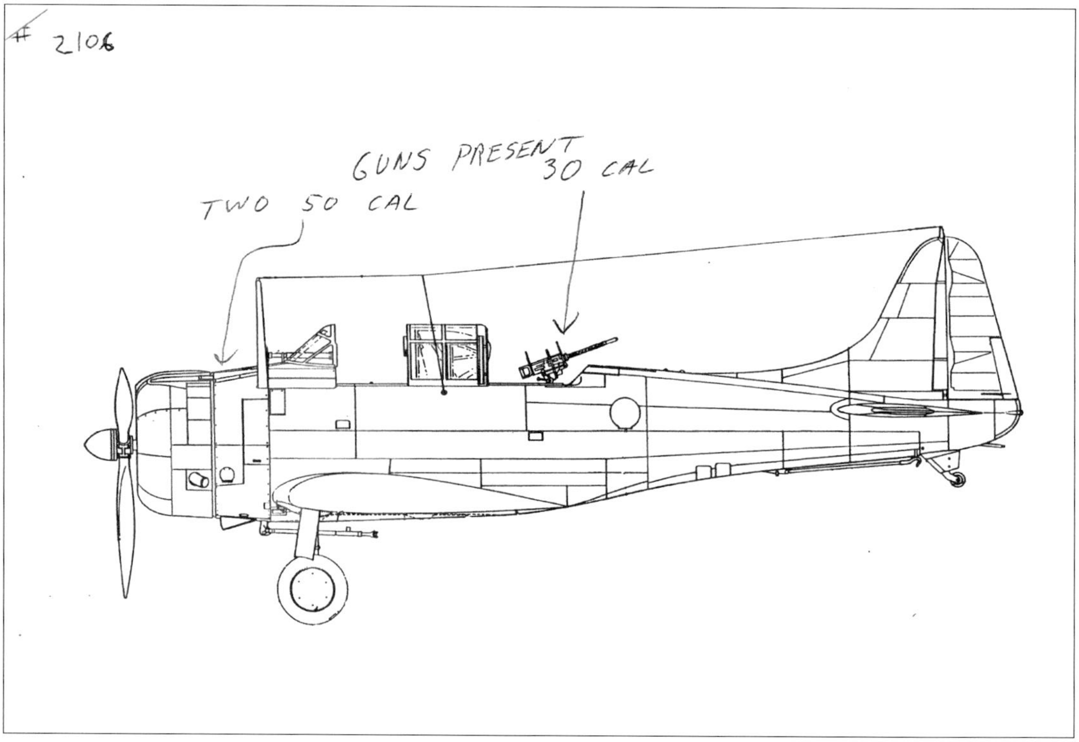

2106

GUNS PRESENT

30 CAL

TWO 50 CAL

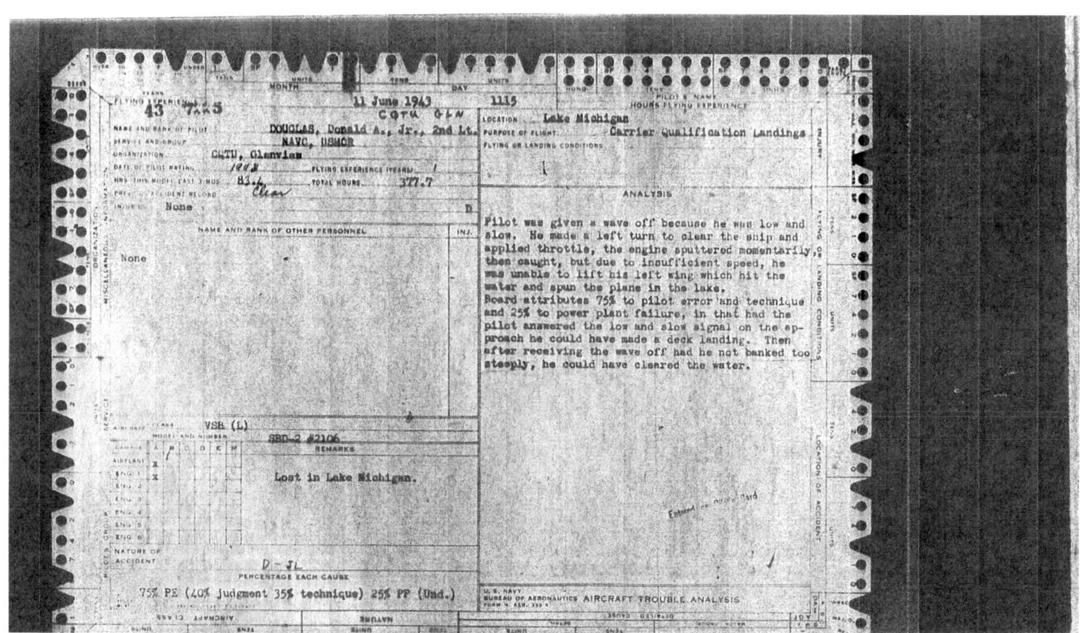

FLYING EXPERIENCE 43 7-25

11 June 1943 1115

CQTU GLN

PILOT'S NAME HOURS FLYING EXPERIENCE

NAME AND RANK OF PILOT: DOUGLAS, Donald A., Jr., 2nd Lt.

SERVICE AND GROUP: NAVC, USMCR

ORGANIZATION: CQTU, Glenview

DATE OF PILOT RATING: 1942 FLYING EXPERIENCE (YEARS): 1

HRS THIS MODEL LAST 3 MOS: 83.4 TOTAL HOURS: 377.7

PREVIOUS ACCIDENT RECORD: Clear

INJURIES: None D

NAME AND RANK OF OTHER PERSONNEL | INJ.

None

LOCATION: Lake Michigan

PURPOSE OF FLIGHT: Carrier Qualification Landings

FLYING OR LANDING CONDITIONS

ANALYSIS

Pilot was given a wave off because he was low and slow. He made a left turn to clear the ship and applied throttle, the engine sputtered momentarily, then caught, but due to insufficient speed, he was unable to lift his left wing which hit the water and spun the plane in the lake.
Board attributes 75% to pilot error and technique and 25% to power plant failure, in that had the pilot answered the low and slow signal on the approach he could have made a deck landing. Then after receiving the wave off had he not banked too steeply, he could have cleared the water.

AIRCRAFT CLASS: VSB (L)

MODEL AND NUMBER: SBD-2 #2106

DAMAGE	A	B	C	D	E	M
AIRPLANE	X	/				
ENG. 1	X					
ENG. 2						
ENG. 3						
ENG. 4						
ENG. 5						
ENG. 6						

REMARKS

Lost in Lake Michigan.

NATURE OF ACCIDENT: D-JL

PERCENTAGE EACH CAUSE

75% PE (40% judgment 35% technique) 25% PP (Und.)

Entered on Pilot's Card

U. S. NAVY
BUREAU OF AERONAUTICS AIRCRAFT TROUBLE ANALYSIS

1

AIRCRAFT NO. 2106 — MODEL SBD-2 — ENGINE MODEL R-1820-32

DATE ACCEPTED — DATE STRICKEN — CONTRACTOR Douglas (El Segundo Div.)

S. O. NO.	SHIPPED	DESTINATION	RECEIVED	ENG. NO.
	RMS tc 12-28-40	San Diego, Batfor.	ar pr tc 12-30-40	4689
	ar pr tc 12-30-40	VB-2, LEXINGTON	ar tc 12-31-40	4689
		P. Hrbr. Batfor	PR 12-5-41 PR	
	AR 12-12-41 PR	VB-2, Lex.		
		P. Hrbr. Batfor	PR tc ar 4-15-42	5123
	tc PR 5-6-42 WAR	CASU-1		
	5-6-42 WAR	VB-3	5-6-42 w	
	ar tc 5-15-42 WAR	P. Harbor, Pac.	tc PR 5-15-42	
	tc war 5-23-42	2nd Marine Aircraft Wing. P.H.		5123
	5-23-42 war	VMSB-241 damaged WAR 6/[illegible]	5-28-42 AR	
	war 6-21-42	Nas. Midway Is.		
	7-3-42 WAR	P. Harbor, Pac.	tc 7-3-42 PR	
	PR tc 7-5-42 WAR	San Diego, Pac.	7-22-42 Dow	5123
		ABG-2	PR 7-22-42	5123
	1-19-43 war	CQTU, Pac.	1-19-43 war	
	WAR [illegible]	CQTU, glenview		

STRICKEN

AIRCRAFT NO. 2106 (Cont over) — MODEL SBD-2 — CONTRACT NO. 65969

2

AIRCRAFT NO. 2106 — MODEL SBD-2 — CONTRACT NO. 65969

DATE	STATION	TROUBLE REPORT – REMARKS
	Con't	
	6-11-43	CQTU Glenview
	9-13-43	STRICKEN

TOTAL FLYING TIME — LOG BOOKS RECORDED

The start of lift of SBD-2 Dauntless dive-bomber, 2106.

SBD-2, 2106, fully out of the water. Clearly visible is the single .30 Browning machine gun the radioman-gunner used to defend the aircraft from enemy fighters.

The beginning of the disassembly and truck loading of Dauntless, 2106. Note the snow. The recovery of aircraft from Lake Michigan is always a cold endeavor—a little bit of snow on the ground is incidental to the crew of A and T Recovery.

Photograph of "Midway Madness." The nickname was stenciled on both sides of the aircraft's engine cowling.

recovery activity. At the beginning of January 1994, we finally received the approval to recover Midway Madness, SBD-2 Dauntless, 2106. Bill Johnson, the director of aircraft restoration for the Naval Museum of Naval Aviation, was sent to work with us, not scuba dive. He had a solid understanding of how an aircraft is recovered from underwater.

SBD-2 Dauntless, 2106, on display at the National Naval Aviation Museum.

10

Recovery Continues with SBD-1 1612

The rule was no aircraft that were war graves would be recovered.

The next aircraft we would recover would be SBD-1 Dauntless, 1612. We had thought for sure that just the mention of recovery of this aircraft would have set the staff at the Naval Historical Center's hair on fire.

On November 21, 1942, the log page of U.S.S. *Wolverine* told a story: "9:50 Fox-8 crashed upon landing, placed on outrigger, 10:38 Fox-7 crashed into the water. YP-532 [Coast Guard rescue boat] picked up the pilot." At 10:50 a.m., the crew of the ship made a course correction and resumed her heading into the wind in order to continue flight operations. The wind was out of the north–northeast, at a force of what they termed as "6." The direction of the wind and the date are very important to understanding what had happened. On that day, the ship's log had no other indication of any aircraft being lost in the lake. However, another aircraft had been lost.

The ship's log pages were not the only place that documented the Navy crashes out on Lake Michigan. The Navy kept records that we term as "accident cards." These short one pagers provide a synopsis of what had occurred concerning aircraft accidents. Early on in our quest for the lost aircraft, we had purchased the microfilm from the National Archives of the accident cards for the tens of thousands of U.S. Navy aircraft of World War II. We went through every one of the records that addressed Wildcats and SBDs, searching for what we liked to call "strays." A stray was an aircraft that had crashed, but was not recorded in the log pages. One of those strays was SBD-1 Dauntless, 1612, which had been lost on November 21, 1942.

What really stood out on the accident card for us was that it stated that the "Plane was observed by a civilian to make a forced landing in Lake Michigan. Neither the body nor the plane have been recovered." That meant it had to be fairly close to shore. However, Chicago's shoreline is nearly 15 miles long, and in order to locate the aircraft, it would help to have some idea of a good starting point. All we really wanted to know was where that "civilian" was standing when he or she saw the Dauntless crash. Since that someone had the wherewithal to contact the Navy's training command with the

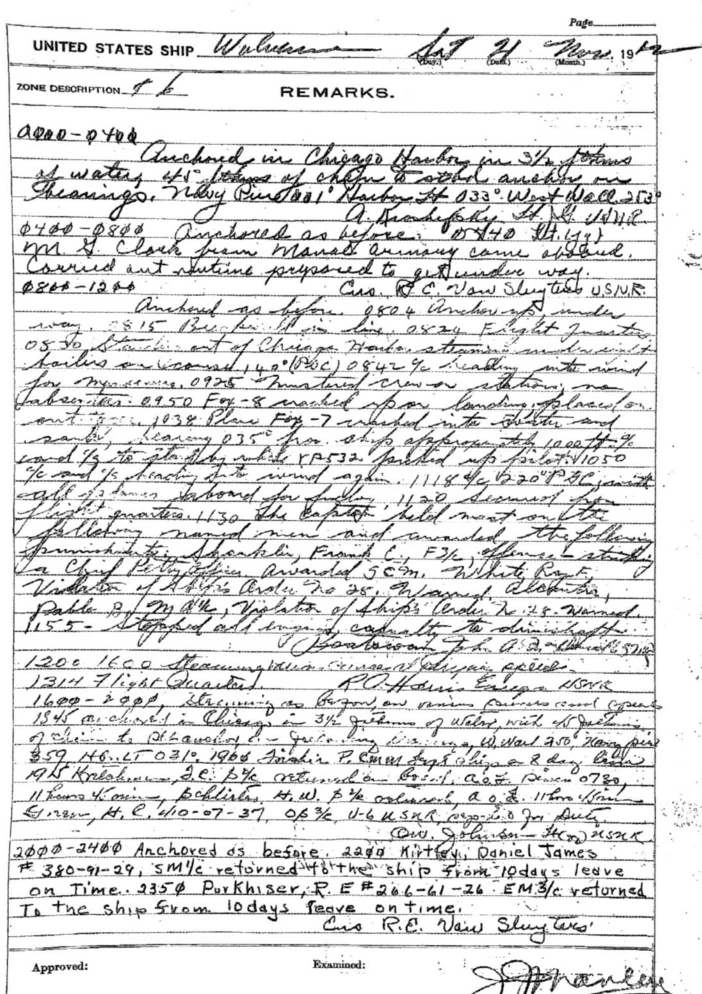

UNITED STATES SHIP Wolverine Sat 21 Nov. 1942

ZONE DESCRIPTION +6

REMARKS.

0000–0400
Anchored in Chicago Harbor in 3½ fathoms of water, 45 fathoms of chain to stbd. anchor on bearings: Navy Pier 001° Harbor Lt 033° West Wall 253°
A. Kondefsky H. G. USNR

0400–0800 Anchored as before. 0740 Lt.(jg) M. G. Clark from Naval Armory came aboard. Carried out routine prepared to get under way.
Ens. R.E. Van Sluyters USNR

0800–1200
Anchored as before. 0804 Anchor up, underway. 0815 ... 0824 Flight quarters. 0830 ... out of Chicago Harbor ... 0842 ... 0925 Mustered crew on stations, no absentees. 0950 F0x-8 ... for landing ... 1038 Plane F0x-7 ... into water and sank, bearing 035° from ship approximately 1000 yds ... while YP532 picked up pilot. 1050 ... 1118 ... 1120 Secured from flight quarters. 1130 The captain held mast on the following named men and awarded the following punishments: Shankle, Frank C., F3/c, offense – striking a Chief Petty Officer. Awarded SCM. ... Violation of Ship's Order No 28. Warned. ... Pablo B., M Att 1/c, Violation of Ship's Order No 28. Warned. 1155 Stopped all engines, casualty to ... shaft.
Boatswain ... USNR

1200 1600 Steaming ... 1314 Flight Quarters.
R.O. Harris Ensign USNR

1600–2000, Steaming as before, on various courses and speeds. 1845 anchored in Chicago in 3½ fathoms of water, with 45 fathoms of chain to stbd anchor ... bearings ... W. Wall 250°, Navy pier 359, H.Lt 031°. 1900 ... 1915 ... returned ... A.O.L. since 0730, 11 hours 45 min ... A.O.L. ...
C.W. Johnson ... USNR

2000–2400 Anchored as before. 2200 Kirtley, Daniel James # 380-91-29, SM1/c returned to the ship from 10 days leave on time. 2350 Porkhiser, R. E # 266-61-26 EM3/c returned to the ship from 10 days leave on time.
Ens R.E. Van Sluyters

Approved: Examined:

U. S. N. Navigator.

Left: The ship's log page of U.S.S. *Wolverine* for November 21, 1942.

Below: The accident card for SBD-1 Dauntless, 1612. Note that there is not a ship named. U.S.S. *Wolverine* would have been the only possible ship, because U.S.S. *Sable* was not in service on November 21, 1942.

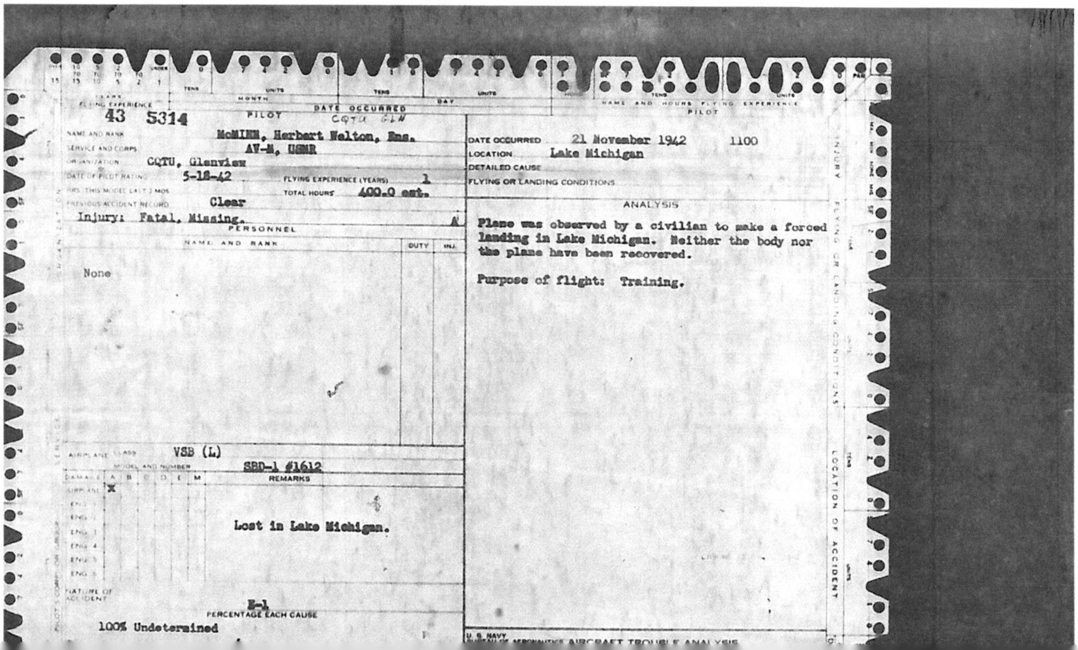

43 5314

PILOT — DATE OCCURRED — CQTU GLN

NAME AND RANK: McMINN, Herbert Welton, Ens.
SERVICE AND CORPS: AV-N, USNR
ORGANIZATION: CQTU, Glenview
DATE OF PILOT RATING: 5-18-42
FLYING EXPERIENCE (YEARS): 1
TOTAL HOURS: 400.0 est.
PREVIOUS ACCIDENT RECORD: Clear
Injury: Fatal, Missing.

PERSONNEL
NAME AND RANK — DUTY — INJ.
None

DATE OCCURRED: 21 November 1942 1100
LOCATION: Lake Michigan
DETAILED CAUSE
FLYING OR LANDING CONDITIONS

ANALYSIS
Plane was observed by a civilian to make a forced landing in Lake Michigan. Neither the body nor the plane have been recovered.

Purpose of flight: Training.

AIRPLANE CLASS: VSB (L)
MODEL AND NUMBER: SBD-1 #1612
DAMAGE: AIRPLANE X

REMARKS
Lost in Lake Michigan.

NATURE OF ACCIDENT: E-1
PERCENTAGE EACH CAUSE: 100% Undetermined

U. S. NAVY ... AERONAUTICS AIRCRAFT TROUBLE ANALYSIS

information about the crash, we figured they must have also contacted the media to tell the story. Within minutes of beginning our search of the microfilm of archived Chicago newspapers, we had our answer. We also knew the general location where Fox-7 had crashed, where its pilot had been rescued, and that the aircraft most likely had been recovered. Fox-7 would have most likely been a Wildcat fighter. The "F" marking on the aircraft was the designator for fighter.

The news articles reported: "Ensign Hebert Welton McMinn, United States Naval Reserve flyer of Gouldbusk, Tx., was reported missing yesterday in an airplane accident over Lake Michigan about five miles off Chicago's north shore"—5 miles from shore seems to be a good distance from shore, but not so far for a healthy twenty-something-year-old to swim. Knowing the direction of the wind and the date are important to providing some understanding to what happened to Ensign McMinn. When the crash occurred, the direction of the ship would have been into the wind. That meant the ship and Coast Guard Rescue boat's "coarse correction" would have sent them heading farther into the lake, leaving the pilot alone to save himself. If Ensign McMinn had crashed in the month of August, the water temperature would have been close to 75 degrees. The young aviator, after having exited the doomed aircraft, would have been pushed by the wind for several hours. He would have reached somewhere close to Chicago's North Avenue Beach, where in all likelihood he would have simply walked out of the water none the worse for wear. However, it was late November and the water was very cold. His dexterity would have been lost within ten minutes, and exhaustion or unconsciousness may have come within thirty.

On March 27, 1994, Al, Scott, and I began our side-scan search for the aircraft. The sonar malfunctioned. After two more days, we located SBD-1, 1612, 5 miles off the north shore of Chicago. I made a quick dive on her to check for one thing, Ensign McMinn. Neither he, his parachute, nor anything of him could be found. A month later, without so much as a comment from the Naval Historical Center, we recovered the aircraft, disassembled her, and put her on a truck. That was the last I ever thought we would see of her. From that time through to the end of 1996, we went on to recover a good number of additional aircraft.

The lift from the water of SBD-1 Dauntless, 1612.

Douglas SBD-3 Dauntless, 06626, during exhibit preparation at the Yankee Air Museum. This aircraft will be displayed very much portraying how she was found on the bottom of Lake Michigan.

Above and below: Lift photographs of SBD-3 Dauntless, 06694, on July 17, 1994. This aircraft can now be seen on display at U.S.S. *Lexington* Museum on the Bay, Corpus Christi, Texas.

SBD-3 Dauntless, 06694, on display at U.S.S. *Lexington* Museum on the Bay, Corpus Christi, Texas.

This aircraft shows evidence of a substantial impact with the water. The accident card stated: "Plane struck the water in a near vertical position on its back."

We located the aircraft standing upright on the lake floor. The accident card also stated that the pilot suffered "two deep cuts on forehead."

Above and below: FM-2 Wildcat, 55052, on display just after completion of restoration at U.S.S. *Hornet Sea*, Air & Space Museum, Alameda, California. They use an artistic lighting array to highlight the restoration workmanship. (*Photograph of courtesy C. J. Machado*)

U.S.S. *Hornet* restoration team member Gary Mathews closing the canopy of the Wildcat. The restoration workmanship is clearly demonstrated in this photograph. (*Photograph courtesy of C. J. Machado*)

Taras Lyssenko with the restoration team of FM-2 Wildcat, 55052, during her dedication ceremony aboard U.S.S. *Hornet* Sea, Air & Space Museum, in August 2017. (*Photograph courtesy of C. J. Machado*)

The beginning of the lift of SBD-5, 36176. Another Dauntless recovered from shallow water, 70 feet deep. Note the missing canopy.

At the depth that this aircraft rested, the velocities of water movement in Lake Michigan produce enough force that the rudder and elevator had become dislodged and moved away from the aircraft.

Visible in the photograph outside of the cockpit near the wing root and along the leading edge of the wing are colonies of zebra mussels.

The pilot's instrument panel of SBD-5 Dauntless, 36176. Zebra mussels had begun to envelop the aircraft. This aircraft can be viewed on display at the Palm Springs Air Museum, California.

This aircraft was sent to the San Diego Air & Space Museum.

The accident card for this aircraft stated: "The pilot made a decelerating approach, received the cut signal, dove at the deck, strike hard and bouncing over the barriers. Then, without applying throttle, he hit the deck near the bow and crashed off the port bow into the water..." That would explain the damage to the port wing. This aircraft is on display at the U.S.S. *Midway* Museum.

As with most of the Wildcats, the magnesium part between the engine and airframe was fully corroded, allowing the engine and propeller to become dislodged.

There were two things we found very unusual with this aircraft: firstly, it was resting upright on its main landing gear and propeller at about a 45-degree down angle in 300 feet of water (the wing damage may have prevented her from inverting); secondly, the remarkable condition of the pilot's headrest as seen in this photograph.

11

The Rewrite of the SecNav Instruction

Three years to add one page.

For A and T Recovery, the change of Title 10 U.S. Code § 2572 and SECNAVINST 5755.1 worked well, but for others, there were problems. It was not anything I studied, but I was told of some incident where a man was severely injured while he and his associates were attempting to fly an aircraft they had received in an exchange from Pensacola Naval Air Station. There was a story of some sort of bribery attempt. The attempt had nothing to do with Captain Rasmussen, Buddy Macon, or anyone from the Naval Aviation Museum Foundation. Additionally, there was a lawsuit filed that, although it was found to be frivolous, somehow ensnared the Naval Aviation Museum Foundation and cost that organization a lot of legal expense. In 1996, the Navy decided to halt all exchanges and redraft and fine-tune the Secretary of the Navy's Instruction.

Prior to the start of the instruction's redraft, we had located two aircraft that the National Museum of Naval Aviation really wished to procure. The first was a Vought F4U-1 "Bird Cage" Corsair—at the time, the only one known to still exist in the world. The other was an original production-run Grumman F6F-3 Hellcat that had a substantial Pacific Air Campaign battle history. At that time, it was our belief that if the SECNAVINST needed a tweaking, it would be helpful to bring forth the exchange to rescue these aircraft.

Three years later, at the end of 1999, SECNAVINST 5755.2 was promulgated. It had a few edits, but for the most part was little more than the original six pages. Anticipating exchanges would again begin in early 1999, we sent a letter to Captain Rasmussen proposing an exchange for the locating, recovery, and delivery of a F6F-3 Hellcat fighter, a F4U-1 Corsair fighter, an assortment of SBD Dauntless dive-bombers, and F4F/FM Wildcat fighters. One day, we would achieve what we were proposing, but not as an exchange. The Naval Historical Center would return with a vengeance to obstruct any proposed exchange.

A. and T. Recovery, Inc.
869 89th Street Ocean
Marathon, Florida 33050

January 20, 1999

Capt. Robert Rasmussen, Director
National Museum of Naval Aviation
1750 Radford Blvd
Suite C
N.A.S. Pensacola, Florida 32508

Re: Trade proposal.

Dear Capt. Rasmussen,

I wish to present to you a proposal to trade the locating, salvage and delivery service of a F6F Hellcat Fighter, a F4U Corsair Fighter and an assortment of SBD Dauntless Dive-Bombers and F4F/FM Wildcat Fighters for equivalent value of used, obsolete or surplus military equipment. These aircraft are located at the bottom of Lake Michigan.

These aircraft would be an enhancement to the Museum's collection. The Hellcat and Corsair fighters are very early models of those aircraft, there by making them significant.

Please keep in mind that recovery of aircraft from the Great Lakes is best preformed during summer months. The weather is most favorable at that time.

Thank you for your time and consideration to this proposal.

Sincerely,

Taras C. Lyssenko
Vice-President

Our letter to Capt. Rasmussen.

12

O'Hare International Airport Wildcat

More of these aircraft should be on display in airports.

Chicago's O'Hare International Airport is named in honor of Lt. Cdr. Edward Henry "Butch" O'Hare. He was the Navy's first fighter ace. Additionally, he was the first service member of the U.S. Navy to be awarded the Congressional Medal of Honor during World War II. He received the medal in recognition of his solo attack on a squadron of Japanese bombers on February 20, 1942. It is believed that his actions saved the U.S.S. *Lexington* aircraft carrier from serious damage or destruction, which would have been inflicted by the approaching bombers. During that engagement, Lt. Cdr. O'Hare piloted a Grumman F4F-3 Wildcat, 4031.

In 1997, a Wildcat Fighter, 12320, was be placed on display at the airport in honor of Lt. Cdr. O'Hare. A and T Recovery had recovered the aircraft that had been restored by the National Museum of Naval Aviation Museum and its foundation. The painting, display, and educational exhibit of the aircraft were funded by Mr. Fred Turner and the McDonald's Corporation. This would be the first of three once-lost Lake Michigan World War II Navy aircraft that Mr. Turner and McDonald's Corporation would be instrumental in presenting to the American public.

13

The Naval Historical Center Comes Back True to Form

It had always seemed to me that in Western Culture surnames are intended to tell some detail of the person.

Our letter of January 20, 1999 to Capt. Rasmussen appeared to have been well received, although it took over a year to see actual movement from the Navy. On April 5, 2000, the Naval Inventory Control Point, Philadelphia (NAV ICP) posted a solicitation (N0038300Y0000) in Commerce Business Daily Online. The subject was 99—Underwater Salvage, Aircraft. The text read: "The Navy is seeking to locate and identify two (2) Navy owned, fresh water submerged aircraft in Lake Michigan. The two (2) aircraft are the F4U-1 Corsair and F6F-3 Hellcat and both are World War II vintage aircraft. The proposal submitted to the Navy shall be for the salvage and recovery of both aircraft...." This appeared to be part of what was to be the method for the execution of the exchange program under the new SECNAVINST. It just looked like we would have to do a bit more paperwork, so what. We immediately responded.

Our discussions soon began with the representative from NAV ICP that led to a letter, dated June 22, 2000, sent by us formally proposing a trade. In that proposal, we sought a number of aircraft, including T-34B Mentors that had been turned over to the National Museum of Naval Aviation by the Navy's recruiting command. The aircraft all had really nice Navy color paint schemes—they were really pretty. On November 7, 2000, the National Museum of Naval Aviation sent a letter to NAV ICP indicating their interest in what we had proposed. By that date, we were well aware that there was not a snowball's chance in hell that the staff at the Naval Historical Center would ever allow the exchange to proceed. At the time, the Center's Director was William S. Dudley.

Over the next four years, the staff at the Naval Historical Center came up with every single bureaucratic maneuver possible to obstruct the exchange and the recovery of the two aircraft. At first, they were unwilling to entertain the idea of any recovery approval, claiming they were conducting a Section 106 review of the entire collection of lost Navy aircraft on the bottom of Lake Michigan. Section 106 of the National Historic Preservation Act of 1966 (NHPA) requires federal agencies to take into account the effects of their

A. and T. Recovery, Inc.
869 89th Street Ocean
Marathon, Florida 33050
305-743-5334
Fax: 305-743-5971

April 6, 2000

Mr. Stephen Van Note
NAVICP
700 Robbins Avenue
Philadelphia, PA 19111-5098

Re: Lake Michigan aircraft salvage, SOL N0038300Y0000

Dear Mr. Van Note,

A.and T. Recovery, Inc. has located and video taped the F4U-1 Corsair and the F6F-3 Hellcat World War II vintage aircraft which are submerged in Lake Michigan. We wish to pursue a contract with the Navy to recover and deliver these airplanes.

Sincerely,

Taras C. Lyssenko
Vice-President

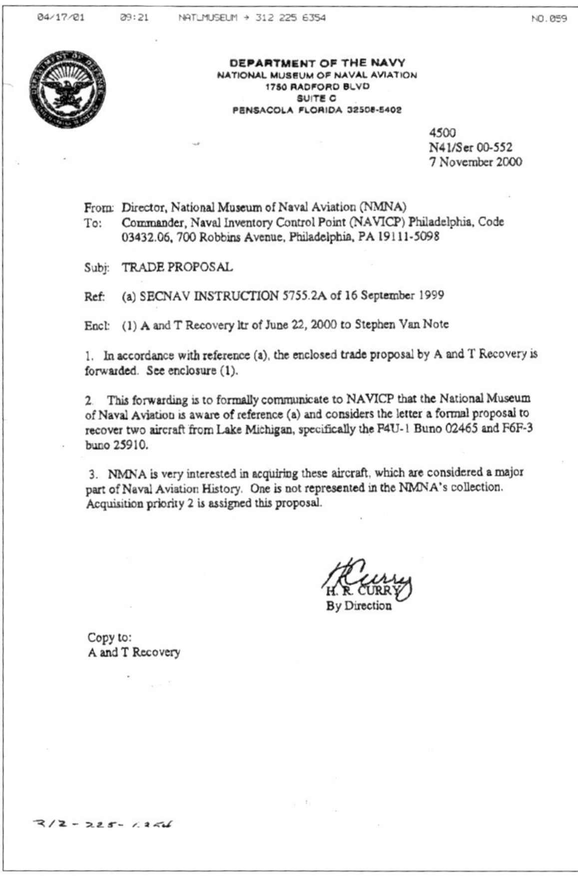

04/17/01 09:21 NATLMUSEUM → 312 225 6354 NO.059

DEPARTMENT OF THE NAVY
NATIONAL MUSEUM OF NAVAL AVIATION
1750 RADFORD BLVD
SUITE C
PENSACOLA FLORIDA 32508-5402

4500
N41/Ser 00-552
7 November 2000

From: Director, National Museum of Naval Aviation (NMNA)
To: Commander, Naval Inventory Control Point (NAVICP) Philadelphia, Code 03432.06, 700 Robbins Avenue, Philadelphia, PA 19111-5098

Subj: TRADE PROPOSAL

Ref: (a) SECNAV INSTRUCTION 5755.2A of 16 September 1999

Encl: (1) A and T Recovery ltr of June 22, 2000 to Stephen Van Note

1. In accordance with reference (a), the enclosed trade proposal by A and T Recovery is forwarded. See enclosure (1).

2. This forwarding is to formally communicate to NAVICP that the National Museum of Naval Aviation is aware of reference (a) and considers the letter a formal proposal to recover two aircraft from Lake Michigan, specifically the F4U-1 Buno 02465 and F6F-3 buno 25910.

3. NMNA is very interested in acquiring these aircraft, which are considered a major part of Naval Aviation History. One is not represented in the NMNA's collection. Acquisition priority 2 is assigned this proposal.

H. R. CURRY
By Direction

Copy to:
A and T Recovery

Above left: Our response to the Navy's Commerce Business Daily posting seeking the recovery of two aircraft from Lake Michigan.

Above right: The internal letter from the National Museum of Naval Aviation to NAV ICP expressing interest in our exchange proposal.

undertakings on historic properties and give the Advisory Council on Historic Preservation (ACHP) a reasonable opportunity to comment. Naval Historical Center's staff sent emails to State Historic Preservation Offices of Illinois and Michigan attempting to get the staff at those offices to make claims of adverse impacts that would result from our recovery of the aircraft. That was an attempt to produce a finding to say the aircraft should not be recovered. Those state offices did not provide the type of the comments the staff at the Naval Historical Center were seeking. Years later, we would learn that they never completed the 106 review. Then there was another claim that the Naval Historical Center was working on an "interagency" agreement with the Great Lakes States concerning management of the aircraft. Similar to the 106 review, the interagency agreement was not drafted.

We were told that we had to secure an "archeological" project permit from the Naval Historical Center. That permit application had to be submitted by a "qualified" archeologist that they had to approve. They made a mistake and gave us a write-up explaining what it took to be qualified. Long before 2000, we had built a relationship with John T Dorwin, Ph.D. Dr. Dorwin's qualifications were far beyond anything the sophomoric bureaucrats at the Naval Historical Center could ever had imagined. There was no choice for them but to approve him. However, they then claimed that they, the staff of the Naval Historical Center, knew the "correct and proper" methodologies that should be used to recover submerged aircraft. They claimed that our methodologies were incorrect. Dr. Dorwin spent great amounts of time and effort trying to explain to these people—who had never seen a recovery of an aircraft—that the use of large barges with cranes out on Lake Michigan was not the best methodology.

When the Naval Historical Center staff lost that debate, they then turned their attention to the value of the exchanges. Exchanges are based on appraised values of the items and services. The Naval Historical Center staff claimed that they were somehow qualified to be the people to make the appraisals for the proposed exchange items. It was really funny that from their point of view, our services seemed to have no value, but the Navy assets were worth their weight in platinum. They achieved their desired result, we could not agree to an exchange. Fast forward to the present day: the T-34B Mentors we had requested in the exchange proposal are still at the National Naval Aviation Museum, but they are now nothing more than corroded piles of scrap metal that have little, if any value.

The inane actions, behavior, and motives of the people at the Naval Historical Center became publicly visible when the head of the Naval Historical Center's Underwater Archeology Branch made the statement: "Think how much more important it will be to recover one in 100 years from now, or 150 years from now, once this generation has died." His statement was published in the *Virginia-Pilot*, August 23, 2004, in an article entitled "Rift Leaves Hundreds of Planes in World's Bodies of Water." The statement proved that all along they had intended to use almost any means possible to prevent us from recovering the aircraft. It also became evident that those people lacked the intellect to be in any position of responsibility when it comes to the affairs that concern the interests of the American public.

The last day for William Dudley as Director of the Naval Historical Center was September 30, 2004. During Dudley's tenure, his staff took great pride in the passage of what was called the "Sunken Military Craft Act." The bill was absolutely one of the most embarrassing pieces of legislation ever passed by U.S. Congress. Because of the law, the United States has to support any claim by foreign governments, such as that of Spain, as to the ownership of cargoes of their ships from hundreds of years ago. Such cargoes included gold, silver, and precious gem stones that the Spanish stole while raping, enslaving, and murdering the people of the Americas.

14
The Invaders Have Arrived

Zebras and quaggas are destructive little creatures.

When we first started our efforts on Lake Michigan in the late 1970s, underwater scuba diving was always hampered by what is termed as "visibility." The lake was known for being cold and dark at any depth beyond two atmospheres. On a good day, we could see 10 feet (3 meters) when on the bottom, even when using underwater flashlights. In the late 1980s, an invader called the "zebra mussel" made its way into the lake. They are filter feeders that did an amazing job of clearing the sediments from within the lake's water column. The lake's visibility became greatly expanded.

Soon, the zebra mussel could be found everywhere in shallow water, covering anything that was stationary, including docks, water intake pipe lines, and shallow water shipwrecks. The biologists told us that the species would not go much deeper than 50 feet, but we were soon to find them on the stumps in the early Holocene Forest at 85 feet deep.

By the early 2000s, the zebra mussels seemed to be covering all the aircraft and shipwrecks shallower than 100 feet. Then we were made aware of the next invader, the "quagga mussel." This was odd to me because a quagga was a subspecies of zebra that had gone extinct. This quagga, although a mussel, does not seem to have any chance at extinction. In fact, they seem to be far more resilient than the original zebra mussel species. These creatures were and still are covering everything to depths of hundreds of feet. It seems they are even able to attach themselves to the lake's floor.

Both species are terribly destructive to the aircraft and shipwrecks. They attach themselves with narrow fibers to almost any and every stationary object. Then they build layer upon layer in their colonies with uncalculatable numbers adding great weight upon wherever they reside, eventually ripping things apart. Additionally, they excrete waste, placing any platform that is their home in a constant acidic bath, which accelerates decay and corrosion.

Stump sample. Note in the center of the photograph there are fully mature zebra mussels.

The instrument panel of the Corsair we would recover in 2010 from 240 feet deep. Healthy adult quagga mussels are well established.

This photograph of a section on the dive brakes of a SBD Dauntless recovered from nearly three hundred feet deep show a substantial quagga mussel colony.

The corrosion visible in this photograph of an area of engine cowl on a FM-2 Wildcat recovered in 2012 is in all likelihood the result of the quagga mussel colony that A and T Recovery's divers had removed.

15

A SBD Dauntless for Midway Airport

It was worth it. That SBD is the most viewed artifact in the Navy's historic collection.

Circa 1998, I visited Capt. Rasmussen and Buddy Macon at the National Museum of Naval Aviation. During our conversation, they mentioned that they had been approached by people in Chicago concerning the placing of a SBD on display in the terminal at Midway Airport. The venue would be very appropriate for such an aircraft since one of the reasons for the airport's name was to honor the men who fought the Battle of Midway. The battle has long been considered the turning point of the war in the Pacific. I thought it was odd that they mentioned it to me. They had never included Al or me in any discussion of where any of the aircraft could, should, or would be displayed. They said that the effort seemed to have stalled. Since I lived in Chicago, I might want to check on the status and perhaps become involved. I am always up for a challenge, so I said that I would look in to it.

It had been my observation that most of the aircraft we had recovered went into museums that have staff who are very accustomed to moving in and out such items for display. They have Boards of Directors that work to raise money to keep their exhibits changing, interactive, and appealing in many ways. Airport terminals are entirely different animals. You cannot just say we want to put this aircraft in here and it magically occurs. I soon came to realize that placing the Dauntless on display within the terminal at Midway International Airport was going to be an expensive, logistically difficult proposition.

I started my involvement by sending a letter to Chicago Mayor Richard M. Daley on January 1, 1999, inquiring as to the status of the effort. Within two weeks, I received a letter from Mary Rose Loney, then Commissioner of the City of Chicago, Department of Aviation. The letter explained:

> Pursuant to a resolution adopted by the Chicago City Council September 9, 1998, the Department of Aviation is in the process of finalizing design plans with an aircraft restoration company for a Battle of Midway exhibit in the new terminal building.

> This exhibit will include a Douglas SBD Dauntless aircraft similar to the one which flew during the Battle of Midway. It will include an educational display about this historic World War II event.
>
> Thank you for your interest in Chicago Midway Airport. I sincerely hope you will visit the new terminal upon its completion to view the Battle of Midway exhibit.

I guess she had not received the memo that the aforementioned "aircraft restoration company" did not have the ability to make the project a reality. Not that I did, but I had a plan. I started building an alliance of individuals and organizations that, if nothing else, showed solid interest. Alderman Edward M. Burke was key to the efforts. He was the powerful Chairman of the Committee on Finance. He also was the Alderman that had presented the City Council resolution requesting a SBD for Midway Airport on loan from the National Museum of Naval Aviation.

Another key individual was the City Aviation Department's managing Deputy Commissioner Erin O'Donnell. She was quick to realize that funding to bring a Dauntless for display at the airport was not available. She did have access to funding for art from a program that was in place as a result of the City's "Percent-for-Art Ordinance." Ms. O'Donnell moved forward with putting in place an exhibit that would include historic photographs and a visual presentation that explained the significance of the Battle of Midway. It is my understanding that photographic images are considered art. Alderman Burke arranged a meeting with Deputy Commissioner O'Donnell where she explained what would be needed to move forward with our effort to hang an actual aircraft in the airport's terminal.

The exhibit Deputy Commissioner O'Donnell was able to build and put in place using the Percent-for-Art Ordinance.

Several of us formed a group that we titled the "SBD Dauntless Dive-Bomber for Midway Committee." At first, we really struggled—it is hard to raise money for historic projects. However, Erin O'Donnell soon played a substantial role in moving our effort forward. Her team had completed the construction of the exhibit for which she had been able to find funding. It is an interesting exhibit that has a hologram depicting the battle along with historical photographs. Deputy Commissioner O'Donnell prepared a dedication ceremony to which she invited dignitaries and others appreciative of the story. She invited me and a really key person to attend, Vice Admiral William D. Houser, USN (Ret.).

At that event, Admiral Houser and I met and spoke. I told him what we were trying to achieve with the installation of an actual SBD Dauntless. He told me that he had an idea of who to bring into the discussion to advance the project, Mr. Fred Turner, Chief Executive Officer of the McDonald's Corporation. It was not long before I was contacted by Lisa Howard, McDonald's Director of Corporate Communications.

Ms. Howard asked that I come to the McDonald's headquarters for a conversation with her and Fred. The visit was a lot of fun for me. The day I visited happened to be the day McDonald's was introducing the "I'm lovin' it" campaign. I had never seen such behind the scenes marketing activities. It was a new experience for me. Most importantly, after the meeting, I knew that the project now had legs and was moving forward.

Fred brought in a man named Joseph Jannotta. Together they went to see Chicago's mayor, Richard M. Daley, in order to gain his support for the effort. They were successful. From there, they went to the CEO of the Boeing Company and the management of the McCormick Tribune Foundation. They were able to secure substantial financial support from both organizations for the effort.

Soon after, Erin O'Donnell introduced me to her project director, Deanna Shoss. Deanna was responsible for making sure all of the "Is" were dotted and the "Ts" were crossed so that the actual moving parts of the project could occur. There had to be an agreement worked out between the National Naval Aviation Museum and the City of Chicago's Department of Aviation. The city's risk management attorneys had to be assured that the aircraft displayed in the airport's terminal did not place the city in any sort of legal jeopardy. Additionally, it was very important that the display of the aircraft and any other associated items would not adversely impact the operations and safety of Midway International Airport.

Deanna enlisted the assistance of Allen Pomerance, Executive Vice President, Aviation Group, A. Epstein & Sons International. Al's team conducted the architectural analysis that was needed to bring in and suspend a SBD Dauntless within the airport's terminal. They also brought Leopardo Companies into the effort.

Capt. Rasmussen had selected a SBD for display, it was Dauntless, 10575. That was the aircraft that had crashed into the early Holocene forest. At the time, the aircraft was painted as an U.S.A.A.F. A-24 Banshee and was on short-term loan to the National Museum of the United States Air Force. The aircraft had to be repainted to the Navy colors of a SBD that would have participated in the Battle of Midway. Also, some modifications of the aircraft were needed to assure the risk management attorneys there would never be a chance the aircraft would become dislodged and fall while on display in the terminal. What is termed as the "Tiger" team traveled to Dayton, Ohio, home of the air force museum. The Tiger team specialized in the hanging of the Navy's historic aircraft. At the air force museum, the team installed a super suspension apparatus in the aircraft with a capability that is many times more substantial than could ever be needed. The attorneys were happy.

In August 2004, all of the funds had been raised, the contracts were signed, every conceivable analysis had been performed, and the aircraft had been modified. She was ready to be transported to Chicago. The "committee" wanted to throw a party, a wonderful idea. One committee member, John Crowley owned a boat storage facility that was for the most part empty at the time, so we brought the SBD there. We bought a bunch of brats from Johnsonville and that company's representative lent us a giant barbeque grill. McDonald's sent over a truck filled with all the other supplies needed and we had a big party. The next day, we brought the aircraft to Midway International Airport.

The Leopardo team took out a wall of the terminal and built a scaffolding that went up several stories. The idea was to lift the aircraft by crane to the top of the scaffold structure, place it on baby crib mattresses, which were placed on top of dollies, then roll the whole assembly through the terminal, about a city block. Everything went fine until we realized that the landing gear would not retract. During the aircraft's restoration, someone had made a bit of a mistake. So there we were, a lot of people, standing on top of a structure that sort of looked like a giant tinker toy, trying to figure out what to do next. Bill Johnson, the National Naval Aviation Museum's Tiger team leader, told me not to give it a second thought because he had seen and repaired every possible thing when it came to these aircraft. His team rounded up a few tools, and in a very short time, they had collapsed the gear. We pushed the aircraft into the building and the Leopardo team closed the wall behind us. Over the next two nights, the Tiger team,

Deanna Shoss and her son, Lucca, with Dauntless, 10575, at the brat party.

Leopardo staff, and A and T Recovery Crew assembled and lifted Dauntless SBD-5, 10575, into place within the terminal at Chicago's Midway International Airport.

The time came to dedicate the aircraft. I told Deputy Commissioner O'Donnell and Deanna that I would bring to the dedication veterans of the actual Battle of Midway. They liked the idea. With the assistance of Southwest Airlines, I flew in about a dozen veterans of the battle, along with their spouses, and put them up in one of the Midway Airport area's hotels. That night, I hosted a big party. Later, I was told that what I did was put together the largest ever reunion of veterans of the Battle of Midway. I have no idea if that is true, but it sure makes for a good story. The following day, the dedication went as planned, with speeches from Mayor Daley, Joseph Jannotta, Capt. Ed Ellis, and Capt. Norman J. "Dusty" Kliess, one of the true heroes of the Battle of Midway.

Reflecting back on the young flippant me during that first conversation with Capt. Rasmussen and Buddy Macon about this project, I thought it would only take a few casual conversations to bring the display of this aircraft to a reality. In the end, it took the involvement of hundreds of people. Beyond our recovery team, there were dozens of restorers, lawyers, elected and appointed government officials, the hundreds who provided funding support, committee support, the construction crews of Leopardo, the group from Epstein, Alderman Burke and his dedicated staff, Erin, Deanna, and their staff, Fred, Lisa, all the other people from McDonald's, and even the guys that grilled the brats were needed to achieve success. SBD-5 Dauntless, 10575, is the most viewed artifact in the U.S. Navy's historic collection. Millions of people every year pass right under her. We did a good thing, and it was well worth the effort.

Dauntless, 10575, on display in the terminal at Chicago's Midway International Airport.

16

Recovery begins again in 2008 under Rear Admiral Jay A. DeLoach, U.S.N. (Ret.)

We can't start until the Hula dancers arrive.

Ken DeHoff

After William Dudley left the Naval Historical Center, the Navy had several "seat warmers" in the position as director. Somewhere along the way, the Center's name changed to the Naval History and Heritage Command. The National Museum of Naval Aviation became the National Naval Aviation Museum. At that time, several other museums came forth and requested aircraft from Lake Michigan, including the National World War II Museum and the Pacific Aviation Museum.

On June 22, 2008, Rear Admiral Jay A. DeLoach, U.S.N. (Ret.), took the helm of the Naval History and Heritage Command. It seemed that he instantaneously brought back the rescue of the Lake Michigan aircraft. By late 2008, we were out on the lake working on the recovery of a Dauntless for the National World War II Museum. In April 2009, we lifted SBD-5 Dauntless, 36291, for the National World War II Museum.

It had been thirteen years since one of the once-lost World War II U.S. Navy aircraft had been recovered from Lake Michigan. For the lift, we invited many very distinguished individuals. Those that came to see that the recoveries had finally resumed included Capt. Grant C. Young, U.S.N. (Ret.), Capt. Charles Downey, U.S.N. (Ret.), Kenneth DeHoff, Executive Director, Pacific Aviation Museum, and Fred Turner, CEO McDonald's Corporation.

It has long been thought that George H. W. Bush was the youngest aviator in U.S. Navy History, but that was incorrect. The youngest known was Charles Downey. During World War II, Grant Young was the Avenger pilot who had put the fatal torpedo into the side of the pride of the Japanese Navy, the battleship *Yamato*. Both men had qualified as aircraft carrier pilots out on Lake Michigan, with Young having survived a ditching in the lake as a result of an engine failure on take-off from the U.S.S. *Wolverine*, December 17, 1943. The aircraft he had been flying was a TBF-1 Avenger, 06064. Over the years, both of these men had become very close friends with us and strongly supported our efforts.

Taras Lyssenko and Keith Pearson studying SBD-5 Dauntless, 36291, preparing to position her on the ground during the lift.

An interesting moment in time caught in a photograph.

SBD-5 Dauntless, 36291, safely on the ground. Notice the different markings that are visible from the aircraft's assignments and history.

Kenneth DeHoff and Fred Turner came because they wanted us to recover a Dauntless for the Pacific Aviation Museum, which is now named the Pearl Harbor Aviation Museum. They seemed to wish to complete a contract and pay for it right then and there. Fred kept asking me how much he needed to write on his check. We greatly appreciated his enthusiasm, but I had no way to know the cost of the restoration, for that we needed to engage the Naval Aviation Museum Foundation. Fred also had several demands for his participation in the recovery and restoration efforts. He explained to us was that he wanted the SBD to be recovered, restored, and painted in the colors of Pacific War hero Admiral James D. "Jig Dog" Ramage.

The two men had no idea of how fortuitous their timing was. We had a Dauntless ready for recovery that would stun even us. It was a real oddity, a SBD-2P Dauntless, 2173. We had located this photo reconnaissance Dauntless variant on May 19, 1993. Al, Scott, and I were on the team that day. The aircraft was near the Wisconsin–Illinois border, which made her the most northern Lake Michigan World War II Navy aircraft we have ever located. Our first sight of her was a pass right over the top, so we had the position without much real effort. On the third pass, the image was so good we did not make another. The scan's "shadow" (white area on the sheet) showed the aircraft intact standing on her nose. We found her quickly that day, as we had searched and covered much of that area the prior day. We continued north and located a civilian Mooney aircraft that had crashed off of Milwaukee. Something to locate just to do it.

Above: From left to right: Capt. Grant Young, Fred Turner, and Capt. Charles Downey at the recovery of the Dauntless for the National World War II Museum.

Right: The side scan sonar image of SBD-2P Dauntless, 2173.

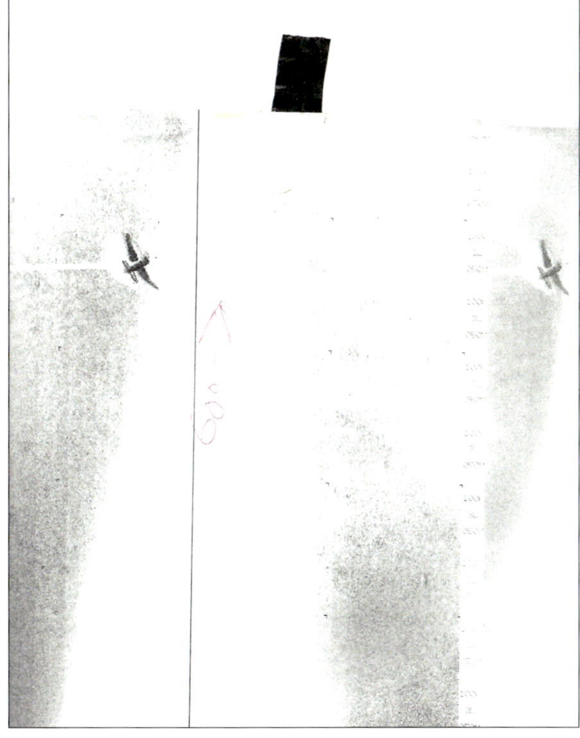

I cannot really say why we did not recover the aircraft during one of the contracts of the 1990s. In all likelihood, Al and I were holding her back as we were with several other aircraft, including a Hellcat and a "Bird Cage" Corsair. We most likely wanted to make sure there would be some real eye catchers in order to bring about more recovery contracts. If that was our thinking, it worked. However, we did take a risk that such aircraft would have been forever lost to time.

After the day of the recovery of the SBD for the National World War II Museum, Fred understood how the funding process works. Funds are donated to the museum of choice, which donates those funds to the Naval Aviation Museum Foundation. The foundation then contracts with A and T Recovery. It actually works very well. Donors get their tax deduction, the museums get their aircraft, and the Navy is insulated from any legal jeopardy, but gets a lot of credit. Fred wrote his check and all the parties began working.

It was not even a month later when a press release was sent out from the Illinois Historic Preservation Agency:

SBD 2173 Recovery Press release

CONTACTS:

June 17, 2009 — Taras Lyssenko, A&T (305) 794-4457
tarasatsea@aol.com

FOR IMMEDIATE RELEASE — David Blanchette, IHPA (217) 558-8970
Dave.blanchette@illinois.gov

U.S. Navy to recover historic World War II airplane from Lake Michigan

WAUKEGAN—A World War II bomber that has been sitting at the bottom of Lake Michigan off the Chicago shoreline for more than 60 years will be brought to the surface this week.

The Pacific Aviation Museum, Pearl Harbor, Hawaii has sponsored the location, recovery, restoration, and eventual display a World War II Douglas SBD Dauntless dive bomber from the depths of Lake Michigan. The National Naval Aviation Museum, in coordination with the Naval History and Heritage Command, the Illinois Historic Preservation Agency and the Naval Aviation Museum Foundation, will complete the recovery portion of the effort this week using a crew from A&T Recovery. This recovery has been made possible through a generous donation from Fred L. Turner of Deerfield, Illinois.

"It is my honor and privilege to support this effort to present, to the American public, this portion of the history of the 'Greatest Generation,' whose courage and love of our country preserved America's and the world's freedom," stated Mr. Turner, "It was their sacrifices which allowed America to become such a great country and provided people such as myself the opportunities to prosper, this is a small thing I have done for the people to whom we all owe so much."

The airplane was lost in Lake Michigan on February 18, 1944. The pilot was Lieutenant Junior Grade John Lendo of Massachusetts. LTJG Lendo later went on to serve in the Pacific Theatre of Operations where he made the ultimate sacrifice in protecting America's freedom.

> The Douglas SBD Dauntless was credited with winning the Battle of Midway and turning the tide of the Pacific war in America's favor. This airplane crashed in Lake Michigan during aircraft carrier qualification training, which was conducted on Lake Michigan during the early to mid-1940s. More than 17,000 pilots completed the training including LTJG George H. Bush, later to become U.S. President. The aircraft carriers used for training docked at Navy Pier in Chicago and the airplanes and pilots flew from Glenview Naval Air Station in Glenview, Illinois. Prior to the activities on Lake Michigan this SBD-2 (Serial No.2173) Dauntless served aboard US Navy Aircraft Carriers USS Enterprise (CV_6) and the USS Yorktown (CV-5).
>
> *more*
>
> The Illinois Historic Preservation Agency, the state government agency that administers all state and federal historic preservation programs in the state, approved the salvage operation. The Agency has jurisdiction over historic resources in Illinois, including those located beneath Illinois territorial waters such as Lake Michigan.
>
> MEDIA ADVISORY: The salvaged airplane will be removed from the water at approximately 10 a.m. Friday, June 19 (weather permitting) at Larsen Marine at Waukegan Harbor in Waukegan, Illinois. News media coverage of this portion of the operation is welcomed, and media should call Taras Lyssenko at (305) 794-4457 for updates. Larsen Marine is located 625 E. Sea Horse Drive at the northern end of Waukegan Harbor, and may be contacted at (847) 336-5456.
>
> Additional contacts:
>
> Capt. Robert Rasmussen, USN (Ret.), Director, National Naval Aviation Museum (850) 452-3604 ext. 3119.
>
> Capt. Ed Ellis, USN (Ret.), Secretary, Naval Aviation Museum Foundation (800) 327-5002.
>
> Kenneth H. DeHoff, Jr., Executive Director, Pacific Aviation Museum 808-754-6871

The press release was only able to tell a fraction of the story of the aircraft. Hill Goodspeed, the historian of the National Naval Aviation Museum, was able to put together a much more comprehensive narrative:

> An early version of the Dauntless, Bureau Number 2173 was delivered to the Navy as an SBD-2P photo-reconnaissance version, of which only 14 were built. It boasts a most interesting history with a few twists and turns. The aircraft's history card notes its acceptance by the Navy in 1941, and assignment to Scouting Squadron (VS) 6 in the aircraft carrier *Enterprise* (CV 6). During its tour with this squadron, the aircraft experienced its first mishap when its main gear collapsed during a landing, damaging the wings. Assigned to Commander, Battle Force aircraft pool at San Diego in August 1941, Bureau Number 2173 was in California on the "Day of Infamy" on 7 December 1941, but the following month found itself assigned to another aircraft pool at Pearl Harbor. It is here that the record-keeping for the aircraft goes astray. While one page of the aircraft history card indicates assignment to Scouting Squadron (VS) 5 in March 1942, the section of the card that details

"Trouble Reports" related to the plane's service bears the entry "Strike. Crashed at sea. Plane sank immediately." The station noted for this mishap is the aircraft carrier *Hornet* (CV 8), and a look at the ship's war diary and aircraft accident reports from the era reveal that on 21 April 1942, an SBD Dauntless made a hard-water landing in the Pacific, the force of the crash causing the plane to sink quickly with the loss of its crew, Lieutenant Gardner D. Randall and Radioman Second Class Thomas A. Gallagher. Though the war diary indicated that the aircraft was an SBD-3, the aircraft accident report identifies the aircraft lost as SBD-2 (Bureau Number 2173).

Despite the fact that the aircraft was recorded lost at sea, the history card of 2173 continues as normal, listing assignment to Bombing Squadron (VB) 5 after the Battle of the Coral Sea followed by time in Carrier Aircraft Service Unit (CASU) 1 and Marine Aircraft Group (MAG) 21. On 1 July 1942, the custody changes to Marine Scout Bombing Squadron (VMSB) 233, which coincided with another entry made in the Trouble Report section of the aircraft's history card—"Request plane be reinstated." In the frantic pace of wartime operations, the SBD lost while operating from the *Hornet* had evidently been erroneously identified as 2173 when further research reveals that in fact it was likely 2179 that was lost. Now "resurrected" from the depths of the Pacific, 2173 remained with VMSB-233 until November 1942, a month before the squadron departed for service on Guadalcanal.

Additional documentation confuses the issue even more, specifically relating to the airplane's service at the Battle of the Coral Sea. The history card states that the airplane was shipped from Commander, Battle Force at San Diego on 3 January 1942, and was not received by Commander, Battle Force at Pearl Harbor until 6 March 1942. It was recorded as being shipped to VS-5 that same day. If these dates are accurate, the airplane could not have been on board the *Yorktown* (CV 5) at Coral Sea because the carrier with VS-5 embarked had departed Pearl Harbor on 14 February 1942. However, according to email correspondence from a number of respected aviation historians and researchers provided by the Pacific Aviation Museum, other official Navy records contradict the history card. Specifically, Commander, Battle Force records point to the fact that 2173 was loaded aboard the *Yorktown* when she stopped at San Diego en route to the Pacific (she arrived on December 30, 1941 and departed on January 6, 1942). It was kept aboard as cargo during the ship's participation in her first combat raids and then assigned to VS-5 through the Battle of the Coral Sea. The above seems plausible, especially with the confusion surrounding 2173's service. Once the actual pages from the Commander, Battle Force records are received, this part of 2173's history can be confirmed.

It is unlikely that 2173 served during the Battle of Midway. All carrier-based bombing and scouting squadrons were equipped with SBD-3s during that battle.

With the more advanced SBD-5 version of the Dauntless ready to join the fleet in early 1943, 2173's days of frontline squadron service were over, the remainder of its time in service spent rotating between Naval Air Stations (NAS) Jacksonville, San Diego, and Glenview, its service at the later station beginning in April 1943 as part of the Carrier Qualification Training Unit (CQTU) operating on board the training carriers *Wolverine* (IX 64) and *Sable* (IX 81) in Lake Michigan. As Lake Michigan aircraft go, 2173 led a charmed life given the fact that in its cockpit were recently winged naval aviators learning how to perform one of the most difficult tasks in all of aviation—landing an aircraft on a moving ship. The airplane operated accident free for nine months in the CQTU until February 18, 1944. On this day, Lt. (junior grade) John Lendo was on approach for a carrier landing when the engine of 2173 began to lose RPMs before completely stopping, the presumed result of carburetor icing. Lt. J. G. Lendo was not injured in the crash.

John Lendo, a Massachusetts native and graduate of Dartmouth College, had over 1,600 hours of accident free flying in his logbook, the result of having served as a flight instructor at NAS Pensacola, following his graduation from flight school in 1942. However, that changed on this winter day as he ditched the Dauntless in the water. While the plane went to the bottom, Lendo was rescued, destined for assignment to fly F6F Hellcats as a member of the newly established Fighting Squadron (VF) 45. On December 14, 1944, while flying a mission from the deck of the light carrier *San Jacinto* (CVL 30), Lendo was declared "missing in action" during a combat mission over the Philippines. His status was changed to "killed in action" the following year, the aircraft he flew just months before his death is a link to one of the lost members of the "Greatest Generation."

At 10 a.m. Central on June 19, 2009, A and T Recovery was set to lift this unique aircraft from Lake Michigan. However, Ken DeHoff asked that we delay the operation, explaining to me, "we can't start until the Hula dancers arrive."

We at A and T Recovery are very good with practical jokes. I thought that Ken was kidding about the Hula dancers, but he was not, and I soon realized he was serious.

AIRCRAFT NO. 2173 — MODEL SBD-2 — CONTRACT NO. 65969

DATE	STATION	TROUBLE REPORT – REMARKS
7-2-41	VS-6 Conf. TR	Landing gear collapsed, flaps bent. Both wings damaged etc. Eng. 5153
4-21-42	Hornet crash report 250127	Strike. Crashed at sea. Plane sank immediately.
July	ComCarPac (information on strike form)	Request plane be reinstated.

LOG BOOKS RECORDED

There are three pages of "history cards" for this aircraft. The second one provides some back drop for the unusual account of this aircraft that Hill Goodspeed spent time researching.

Ken was really making the best out of the aircraft's history of having been stationed at Pearl Harbor. He brought in three Hula dancers and a priest to bless the Dauntless. At various stages of the lift, we halted so the priest could say a Hawaiian blessing and then the dancers would perform specific movements.

The condition of SBD-2P Dauntless, 2173, was stunning. News articles quoted me as describing the aircraft as "pristine." In relation to most of the recovered aircraft, she was. We joked that all we had to do was change the oil and start her up to fly her to Pensacola. However, we did have to send her by truck to the National Naval Aviation Museum. Once there, she was to undergo an extensive restoration conducted through an agreement between the Pacific Aviation Museum and the Naval Aviation Museum Foundation. However, the restoration did not occur as a result of some unforeseen circumstances. The plan had been to immediately begin the three- to five-year restoration just after recovery. Upon completion of restoration, the aircraft was to be shipped to the Pacific Aviation Museum for display. Another restored SBD was shipped for display until 2173 was completed. Seven years later, I would learn that the aircraft had been barely touched.

Hawaiian priest presents his initial blessing of SBD-2P Dauntless, 2173.

Right: Lone Hula dancer performs after the initial blessing.

Below: SBD-2P Dauntless, 2173, fully out of the water. Note that A and T Recovery's divers have tied the aircraft's tires and inner tubes to the landing gear struts.

Hula dancers perform final dance after the lift of the Dauntless.

Casey people watching after the lift of SBD-2P.

Above left: A tire and inner tube from the aircraft. Note the good condition.

Above right: Starboard landing gear strut of the aircraft. Note that Douglas used cast magnesium wheels on Dauntless aircraft. Those wheels became the aircraft's "anode slaves" and corroded to nothing many years ago.

A and T recovery archeologist John T Dorwin, Ph.D., begins his survey of the aircraft.

The underside of the starboard wing. Note some of the red paint of early war markings can be seen in this photograph.

Group photograph with Hula dancers and Hawaiian priest. Present are Keith Pearson, Kenneth H. DeHoff, Jr. (Executive Director, Pacific Aviation Museum), Taras Lyssenko, Mike Shield (crane operator), and Casey.

17

A Helldiver in the Lower Otay Reservoir

The Navy did not have a SB2C in its historic collection.

Sometime *circa* early 2009, while crossing Lower Otay Reservoir outside of San Diego, California, a freshwater sport fishermen, Duane Johnson, noticed an aircraft on the display of his Hummingbird fish locator. The aircraft was a SB2C-4 Helldiver, 19866. Nearly seventy-five years earlier, on May 28, 1945, the airplane had completed a practice dive-bombing run when it suffered a complete engine failure. After repeated attempts to restart the engine, the pilot, Ensign E. D. Frazar, maneuvered the plane away from the rough terrain around the target area and made a successful "wheels-up" forced-landing in Lower Otay Reservoir. Both Frazar and his passenger in the rear cockpit, Army Technical Sergeant Joseph M. Metz, escaped from the aircraft and swam to shore, the aircraft sinking to the bottom.

The aircraft is an example of the wartime dive-bomber designed by the Curtiss-Wright Corporation. Accepted into the Navy's inventory on July 25, 1944, this aircraft was delivered to San Diego and assigned to Bombing Squadron (VB) 84 in early 1945. A short time later, it was reassigned to Bombing Squadron (VB) 14, the squadron in which it was flying at the time of its ditching. It is one of only six known examples of the SB2C Helldiver still in existence today out of more than 7,100 built.

After Mr. Johnson located the aircraft, he informed the Navy and others as to what he had found. Identifying that the U.S. Navy did not have a SB2C in its historic collection, Capt. Rasmussen set out to have this one retrieved and asked that A and T Recovery perform the recovery. A supporter, Mr. Marlin Overholt, of the National Naval Aviation Museum had recently passed away, leaving the Foundation his estate in order to provide funding for such efforts. It took until August 2010 for all the permits, permissions, agreements, and every other possible discussion to occur in order for us to begin the recovery effort. However, we at A and T Recovery had not been allowed input into those discussions.

Once we began the recovery, we soon realized that there would be a lot of restrictions placed upon us. The one that would be the most troublesome was that the City of San

Sonar image of SB2C-4 Helldiver dive-bomber, 19866, at the bottom of Lower Otay Reservoir.

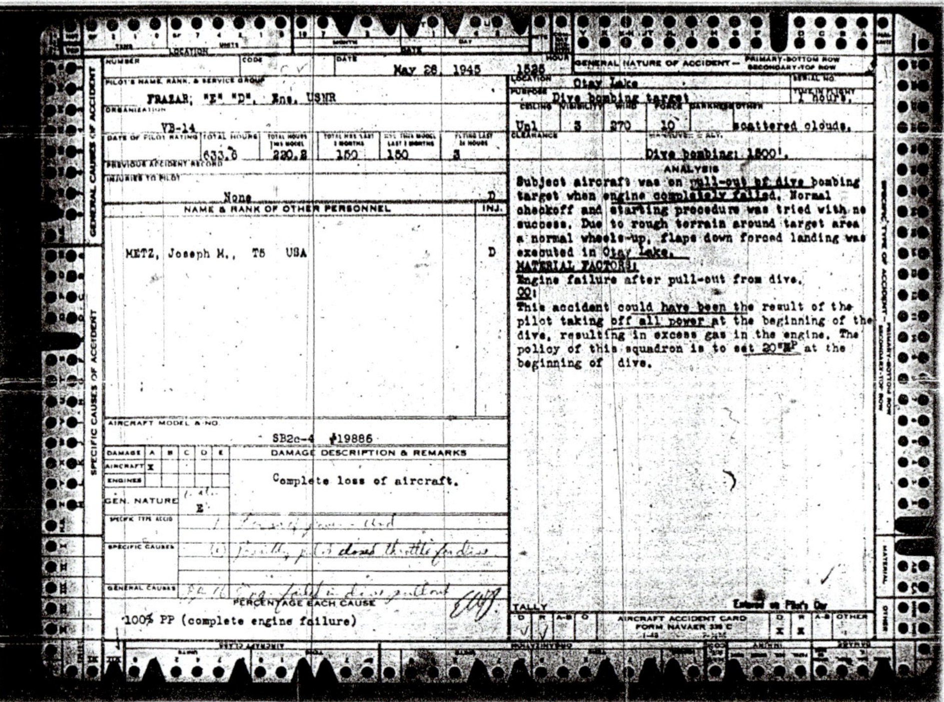

DATE: May 28, 1945 HOUR: 1525

PILOT'S NAME, RANK, & SERVICE GROUP: FRAZAR; "E" "D", Ens. USNR

ORGANIZATION: VB-14

DATE OF PILOT RATING	TOTAL HOURS	TOTAL HOURS THIS MODEL	TOTAL HRS LAST 3 MONTHS	HRS THIS MODEL LAST 3 MONTHS	FLYING LAST 24 HOURS
	633.6	220.2	150	150	3

PREVIOUS ACCIDENT RECORD

INJURIES TO PILOT: None D

NAME & RANK OF OTHER PERSONNEL	INJ.
METZ, Joseph M., T5 USA	D

AIRCRAFT MODEL & NO.: SB2c-4 #19886

DAMAGE	A	B	C	D	E
AIRCRAFT	X				
ENGINES					

GEN. NATURE: E

SPECIFIC TYPE ACCID

SPECIFIC CAUSES

GENERAL CAUSES

DAMAGE DESCRIPTION & REMARKS: Complete loss of aircraft.

PERCENTAGE EACH CAUSE: 100% PP (complete engine failure)

GENERAL NATURE OF ACCIDENT — PRIMARY-BOTTOM ROW SECONDARY-TOP ROW

LOCATION: Otay Lake

PURPOSE: Dive bombing target

TIME IN FLIGHT: 1 hours.

CEILING	VISIBILITY	WIND	FORCE	DARKNESS	OTHER
Unl	3	270	10		scattered clouds.

CLEARANCE

ALT.: Dive bombing: 1800'.

ANALYSIS

Subject aircraft was on pull-out of dive bombing target when engine completely failed. Normal checkoff and starting procedure was tried with no success. Due to rough terrain around target area a normal wheels-up, flaps down forced landing was executed in Otay Lake.

MATERIAL FACTORS:

Engine failure after pull-out from dive.

CO:

This accident could have been the result of the pilot taking off all power at the beginning of the dive, resulting in excess gas in the engine. The policy of this squadron is to set 20"HP at the beginning of dive.

TALLY

AIRCRAFT ACCIDENT CARD FORM NAVAER 339 C

This is the correct accident card for the Helldiver that had crashed in Lower Otay Reservoir. The bureau number was typed incorrectly. On the card, it indicates number 19886, but this should have been 19866.

Diego would only allow us to work within a time frame that they considered the work day, sort of a nine to five thing. They were really good at being bureaucrats and not understanding there is a lot more to recovery operations than what fit into their idea of a perfect world. I could not get through to them the simple concept that once we begin lifting the aircraft we do not stop because it is 5 p.m. I was curious as to how police and firefighters do their jobs in San Diego with such people in charge of the city. After a few days, I found out the person who the city had placed in the position to "oversee" our activities was the city's library director. I met with him several times, but realized he had no concept of what we were doing. It seemed to me that he really did not want the responsibility the city had given him. He kept demanding that we put out more oil boom. I demonstrated to him that we had put in place about twenty times the oil absorption capacity that we would have needed if the aircraft had just crashed. He also refused to believe me that the oil had leaked from the aircraft many years earlier. Additionally, he could not seem to understand the difference between aircraft engine oil and aviation fuel.

When some of the local media asked how long I thought it would take for us to recover the Helldiver, my response was "several days." That was before I knew the city's restrictions. However, the reason I felt it would take even that long was that the bottom of the reservoir has an anoxic layer of decaying organic scum. Over the years, a methane-producing black oozing muck had developed about a 10-foot-thick layer that almost enveloped the entire aircraft. That layer was completely void of light, pitch black, which really diminished the divers' abilities in movement and even minor tasks. We had to remove as much of the material from inside the aircraft and off the wings as possible for the lift. While removing the muck from the pilots' cockpit, the divers found what was truly a wonderful surprise. The parachute was still on the pilot's seat and it was in an almost pristine condition. A short time later, the life raft was located. Both items seemed as if they had only been underwater for a few months rather than decades.

Usually when recovering an aircraft, we put out a press release a day or two before the final lift from the water. The media does not have a clue that it is happening until the aircraft is at shore ready at the lift out point. Is this case, they had been informed at the beginning of the week when we began working. The media was there every single day, what seemed to be all day asking for the latest scoop on progress. Although I would explain to them each procedure of the recovery, the newspaper articles starting having phrases such as "recovery is delayed." I guess they felt that was more interesting to readers rather than saying there is a lot of muck that has to be removed and moved in order to raise the aircraft.

Another situation that was new for us was the large number of people who appeared at the recovery site to spectate. Joseph Metz, the backseat passenger that went swimming with the Helldiver, his brother, and nephew came out to see the recovery. The pilot's son, daughter in-law, and granddaughter, Mr. and Mrs. Richard Frazar, and Allison Davis flew their small plane to San Diego for the event. The California Historic Preservation Officer, Milford Wayne Donaldson, drove down from Sacramento. Even Capt. Rasmussen flew in. They along with what would end up being hundreds of people were there for the lift. They brought coolers loaded with drinks, which gave me the feeling that we were hosting one grand party.

At the time, the Navy was gearing up to celebrate the 100th anniversary of U.S. Navy aviation. Capt. Richard Dann, Executive Director of the Centennial of Naval Aviation,

A close-up underwater photograph of the SB2C's bureau number stenciled on the aircraft's vertical stabilizer.

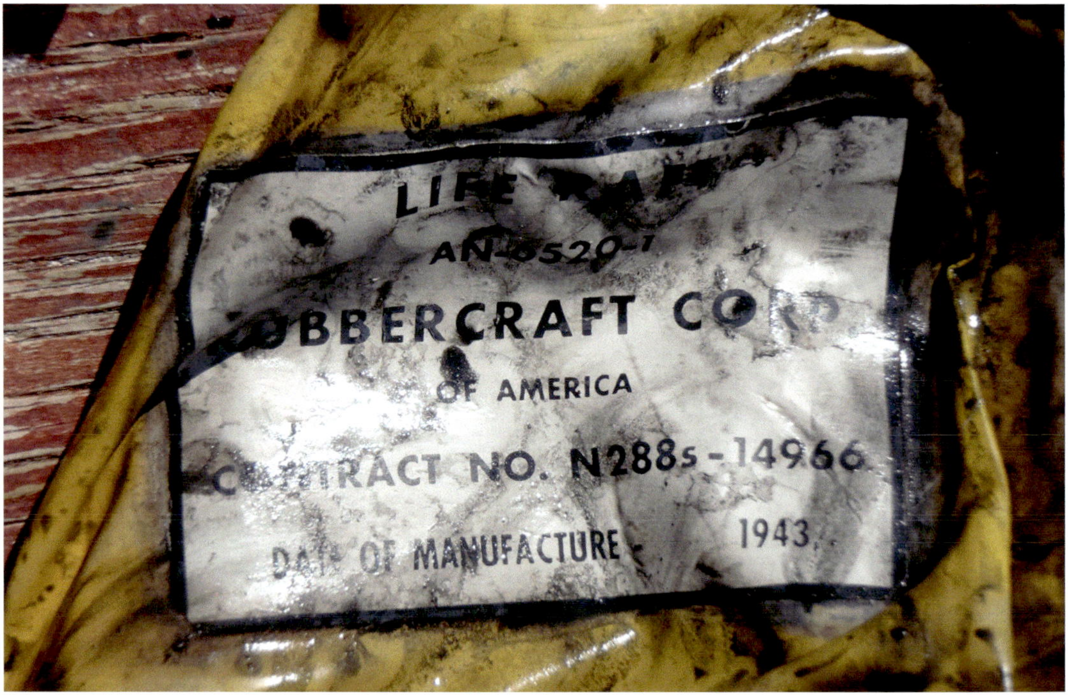

The manufactures label for the Helldiver's life raft.

Aircraft recovery is actually very mundane work as seen by the expression on Capt. Rasmussen's face. In this photograph, he is taking a boat ride along with Todd Brown and Taras Lyssenko just after the retrieval of a section of the Helldiver's canopy.

The Helldiver's canopy laid out for display to the media. It was in very good condition.

had been given the responsibility nationally to arrange and promote the activities over the coming year honoring the men and women who had been successful at protecting the world's freedom and liberty. He happened to be in San Diego for the lift where he was able to locate Navy personnel volunteers who provided us with crowd control support and other valuable assistance.

The most significant factor that made the recovery of Helldiver SB2C-4, 19866, a success was the invaluable support from the City of San Diego's Public Utilities Department Ranger divers. We were displaced from our vessels and a lot of equipment, and our dive and support team was minimal because of the distance from our home base. The Ranger dive team provided a dive barge, other boats for transportation and logistics, a tremendous diving effort, and good old-fashioned manpower that really overcame all of A and T Recovery's shortcomings and weaknesses of that week. Their team consisted of Nelson Manville, James Miller, Kevin Kidd-Tackaberry, Patrick Walter, and Mark Miller. Even one of the Ranger's daughters, Jasmine, supported in the role as my executive assistant and close photo documentarian during the final lift.

The start of the lift Helldiver SB2C-4, 19866, from Lower Otay Reservoir. (*Photograph courtesy of Jasmine Miller*)

The SB2C over land. Taras Lyssenko appears very wary of the aircraft's engine and propeller as it is no longer attached to the airframe. (*Photograph of courtesy Jasmine Miller*)

The aircraft about to be set on the ground. Keith Pearson and Taras Lyssenko studying, discussing, and preparing to deal with the dislodged engine and propeller. (*Photograph courtesy of Mark Miller*)

The aircraft's instrument panel just after recovery. Although a good amount of the sediment from the reservoir had been removed from the aircraft's cockpit, a remaining layer of the material is seen covering everything that is visible in the photograph. (*Photograph courtesy of Mark Miller*)

The group photograph of the team. Capt. Dann, his Navy volunteers, City of San Diego's Public Utilities Department Ranger divers, and A and T Recovery crewmembers, including Keith Pearson, Todd Brown, Pete Spear, and Paul Ehorn. Al and Francis "Bud" Brain skipped the photo, camera shy. (*Photograph courtesy of Jasmine Miller*)

Taras Lyssenko and his trusted executive assistant Jasmine Miller. (*Photograph courtesy of Mark Miller*)

18
Hellcat

Sometimes the media performs an actual act of kindness.

Of all the aircraft recoveries conducted by A and T Recovery, the two that the Naval Historical Center/Naval History and Heritage Command put the most effort into obstructing were the "Bird Cage" Corsair, 02465, and F6F-3 Hellcat, 25910. Their efforts had a lasting effect that even years later would cause us to have to put an unimaginable effort into over coming. It would take years for us to actually find out the lengths to which they had gone to try thwart us.

Circa 2006, Capt. Charles "Ed" Ellis, U.S.N. (Ret.), the relationship builder at the Naval Aviation Museum Foundation, contacted me to tell me Andy Taylor, CEO and Chairman of the Board of Enterprise Holdings, wished to fund the locating, recovery, restoration, and public display of a Hellcat from Lake Michigan. The first thing I asked was if he thought we could overcome the resistance of the Naval History and Heritage Command. His response was that we had to try. Admiral DeLoach would do it for us, but little did we know what else was coming.

Enterprise Holdings is the parent company of Enterprise Rent-A-Car. Both were founded by Jack Taylor, father of Andy Taylor. As a young man, Jack had joined the Navy and had become a decorated aviator flying Hellcat fighters, serving aboard several aircraft carriers, including the U.S.S. *Enterprise* (CV-6). In honor of that experience, he named his company after the U.S. Navy's most decorated ship.

It was Andy's wish to honor the fantastic life of his father and the other men who had served aboard the *Enterprise*. There was perhaps no better way of honoring them than to preserve and present to the American public one of the most magnificent aircraft that had been a workhorse in winning the Pacific War.

The only Hellcat that was still in Lake Michigan was 25910. The aircraft rested in the waters of the State of Michigan. I began the permit process in the autumn of 2008, after we knew we would be able to secure Admiral DeLoach's approval. The first thing I did was to contact the Permit Evaluation Branch A, Regulatory Office, Army Corps of Engineers, Detroit District. On Wednesday, October 9, 2008, I received the following email:

Mr. Lyssenko,

I am writing to follow up our phone conversations of yesterday and today. As I indicated, a new permit application will be required, since the previous application was withdrawn almost four years ago, and the original permit expired prior to that. You may find our joint permit application with the State of Michigan at the following link: http://www.michigan.gov/deq/0,1607,7-135-3307_29692_24403-67347--,00.html I recommend sending a copy of your application to the Corps and to the State of Michigan so both agencies can start their review.

As requested, enclosed is a copy of your application submitted in 2004. I have also included correspondence related to review of the 2004 application, as the issues mentioned remain important to our review. As we discussed, the Corps of Engineers will need to comply with the Section 106 process if a review hasn't been completed already. I understand your concern about the location information, and we will work with you to resolve that.

Once we receive an application, it will be assigned to one of my staff. If you have further questions, please contact me.

Charles M. Simon
Chief, Permit Evaluation Branch A
Regulatory Office
Corps of Engineers, Detroit District

What this person sent was a very nicely worded email that said one thing to me, he was going to do everything he could to obstruct. I had dealt with this person before. In the documents he had attached were letters signed by both William Dudley and one of his underlings from the Underwater Archeological Branch. In one of the letters, dated April 12, 2001, Dudley wrote: "The Naval Historical Center (NHC) is in the process of completing its Section 106 compliance regarding the National Museum of Naval Aviation's (NMNA) proposal for recovery of two World War II era aircraft wrecks owned by the Navy from Lake Michigan…" He went on to explain those aircraft were the F4U-1 "Bird Cage" Corsair and this Hellcat. In another letter signed by the "Acting Branch Head" of the Underwater Archaeology Branch referring to the Hellcat, it was stated: "This aircraft was the subject of an earlier Section 106 review that found it had possible connections to the Solomon Islands campaign in World War II. At the time of the review it was decided that because no definitive connection with the battles could be found, the Hellcat could be raised."

My question was why the Corps of Engineers' person would mention a Section 106 review process in his email. The documents he forwarded to me said it had been completed. The answer would soon become very clear. When we asked the still remaining staff left from the Dudley regime, at what was now the Naval History and Heritage Command, for the documents of the Section 106 reviews, they claimed there were no such documents. All that paperwork had suddenly become nonexistent. No one there had any idea of what we were talking about—even after we presented them with copies of the signed letters. There was no doubt in my mind that this Army Corps of Engineers' person was in contact with staff at the Naval History and Heritage Command. He knew we would find nothing.

In actuality, the Section 106 review was not the responsibility of the Army Corps of Engineers. The aircraft is property of the Navy. The project was that of the National Naval Aviation Museum, it was their or the Naval History and Heritage Command's responsibility to conduct any 106 review. Mr. Simon found other ways to delay granting the permit for over a year. After several less-than-cordial conversations between me and the general counsel and others from the Detroit District of the Army Corps of Engineers, I had enough. In early November 2009, I telephoned the Inspector General of the Army Corps of Engineers. After several colorful discussions with his staff, I received a return call from the actual inspector general. The first things he let me know is that he appreciated me bringing the situation to his attention and that he found my colorful language a bit refreshing. After speaking with me for a short time, he said he would take a look at what I was saying and get back to me. I have no idea what he did or who he spoke with, but a short time later that day, he called me again and told me the permit was on its way.

On November 30, 2009, we lifted the Hellcat. The Enterprise people made a real party out of it. They flew in a bunch of friends of the Taylor family, had it catered, and hired a professional photographer. I had funded the trip for the grandson of the pilot who had crashed with the aircraft to be present at the lift. Fox News did something that really impressed me: they sent crews to both the lift site and to the retirement home where the pilot, Walter Elcock, resided. It was the first and only time I had seen during all of the recoveries where the media was able to interview one of the pilots during the lift of an aircraft. They were able to capture his actual reactions to seeing that portion of his life presented on national television. They did a good thing.

We shipped the aircraft to Pensacola. Four years later, the aircraft's restoration was complete. On Friday, December 6, 2013, the National Naval Aviation Museum hosted a dedication ceremony. Jack Taylor, former naval aviator and great American businessman, was able to attend.

The start of the lift from the water of F6F-3 Hellcat, 25910. Most of the quagga mussels on the outer skin of the aircraft have been removed by the divers of A and T Recovery, but there are many still visible.

Andy Taylor and several of his associates take a close look at the aircraft during a brief pause in the lift. A lot of time is allotted during the lift in order to allow water to drain from the aircraft.

Taras Lyssenko's trusted hound, Casey, performing one of her tasks of inspecting the aircraft during the final lift.

A few moments before the Hellcat is set upon land in nearly sixty-five years. Notice the dense layer of quagga mussels on the underside of the port wing and fuselage.

The F6F-3 about to be set on her landing gear.

F6F-3 Hellcat, 25910, roll out just after restoration by the team of the National Naval Aviation Museum and the Naval Aviation Museum Foundation.

F6F-3 Hellcat, 25910, at the dedication ceremony with a volunteer sailor dressed as the young Ensign Jack Taylor. (*Photograph courtesy of Donald Watson*)

F6F-3 Hellcat, 25910, dedication ceremony group photograph with Jack Taylor, Mrs. and Mr. Andy Taylor, their daughters, the restoration team, and other staff of the National Naval Aviation Museum and its supporting foundation. (*Photograph courtesy of Mike O'Connor*)

19

A "Bird Cage"

That should not be here.

The log page for the U.S.S. *Wolverine* of June 12, 1943 read: "1725 F-21 crashed over port beam into water. Pilot Ensign C Johnson Recovered by crash boat sustaining only superficial cuts. Plane sank in 220 FT water. Marker buoy dropped." To us, that indicated that a Wildcat Fighter would have been lost at that time. After searching all the F4F-3, F4F-4, FM-1, and FM-2 accident cards, we came up empty-handed as to which aircraft it could be. We knew that there had been Hellcats used for the qualifications, but again we came up short after searching those records. That left us with Corsairs and an accident card that was a surprise, although a very pleasant one.

We had always been told the U.S. Navy rejected the idea of F4U-1 "Bird Cage" Corsairs when it came to aircraft carrier operations. Our understanding was that upon attempting to land, the configuration of the cockpit did not allow the pilot a view of the landing signal officer. It was after canopy, other modifications, and the Royal Navy figuring out that the pilots should not square off a base leg that these aircraft could be safely landed on carriers. By continuing to bank until landing, the pilots could maintain the views they needed. We had no idea why any pilot conducting aircraft carrier qualifications would have been sent in such an aircraft to attempt to land on the U.S.S. *Wolverine*. The ship was much shorter and harder to land on than the fleet carriers. The accident card said it all: "Pilot made normal approach, but lost sight of the landing signal officer and did not see the cut signal…" Someone had made a serious mistake back in 1943 by sending that pilot out with this aircraft, but it was to our, the National Naval Aviation Museum, and the people of the United States' benefit. Too bad the marker buoy was not still at the crash site.

In order to find the aircraft, Al again did his charting thing, but this time he did it differently than he had with the U-boat. He followed depth contour lines centered on 220 feet of water. We began intensely searching for the Corsair in May 1995, which I logged as "searched for strays." On July 7, 1995, we hit one of the oddest sonar returns I have ever seen, but we knew it had to be the Bird Cage. It did not reflect the

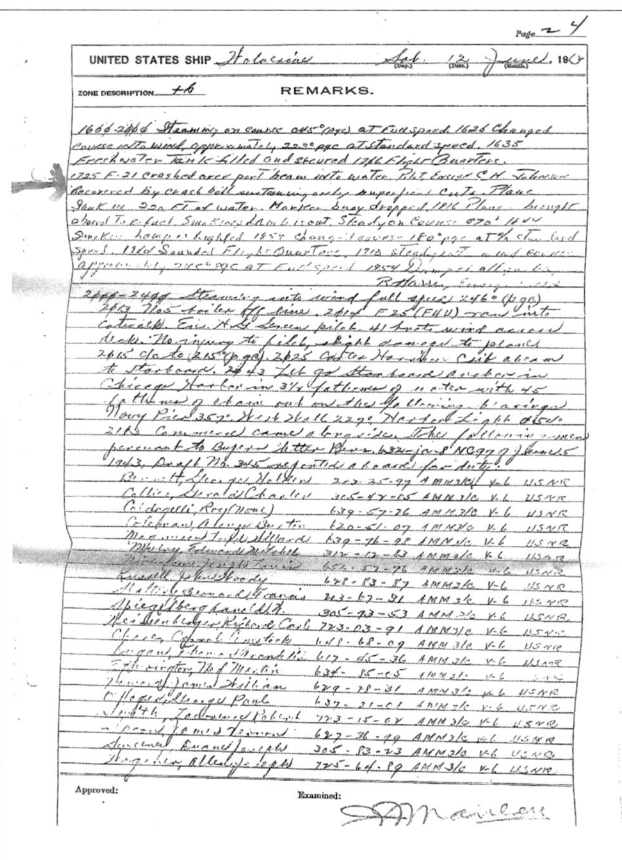

Page 24

UNITED STATES SHIP Wolverine Sat. (Day.) 12 (Date.) June (Month.) 1943

ZONE DESCRIPTION +6 REMARKS.

1600-2000 Steaming on course 045° (pgc) at full speed. 1626 Changed course into wind, approximately 220° pgc at standard speed. 1635 Freshwater tank filled and secured. 1700 Flight Quarters.
1725 F-21 crashed over port beam into water. Pilot Ensign C.H. Johnson recovered by crash boat sustaining only superficial cuts. Plane sank in 220 ft. of water. Marker buoy dropped.

Approved:

Examined:

Left: The ship's log page Saturday, June 12, 1943. Not much there to base a search on.

Below: The accident card for Vought F4U-1 Corsair, 02465, clearly showing that it was, in fact, the F-21 that crashed off U.S.S. *Wolverine* on June 12, 1943.

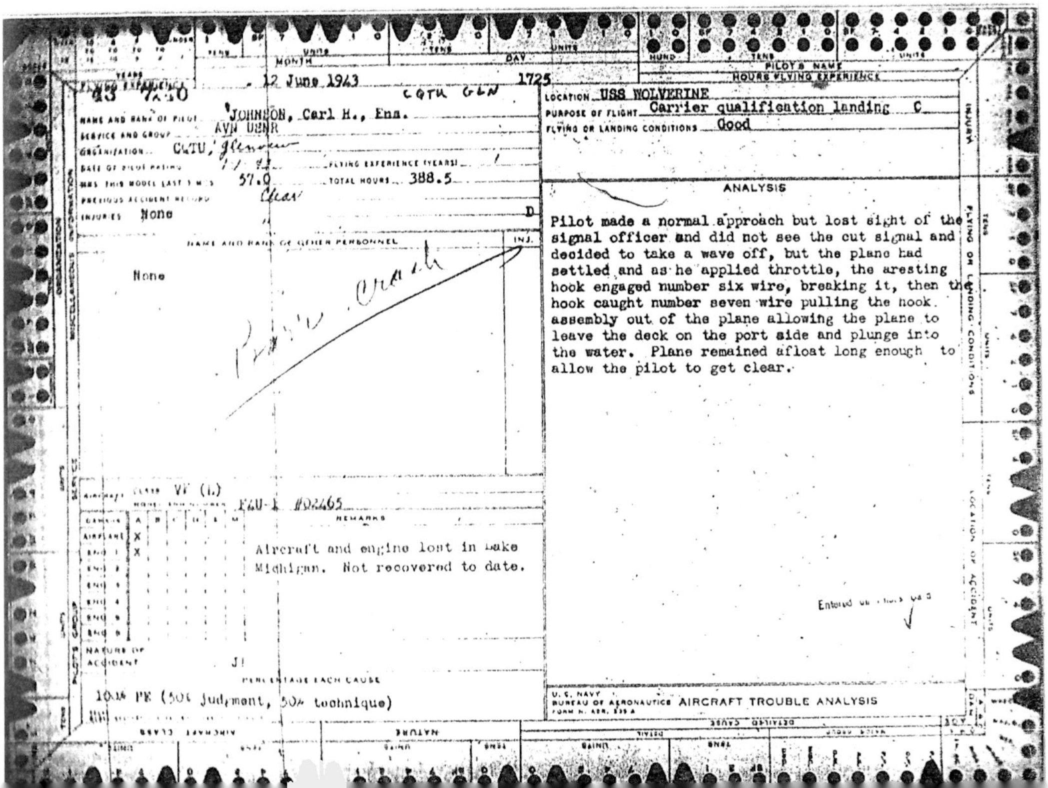

MONTH DAY

YEARS FLYING EXPERIENCE 43 7A30

12 June 1943 1725

CQTU GLN

NAME AND RANK OF PILOT JOHNSON, Carl H., Ens.

SERVICE AND GROUP AVN USNR

ORGANIZATION CQTU, Glenview

DATE OF PILOT RATING 1/ 42

FLYING EXPERIENCE (YEARS) 1

HRS. THIS MODEL LAST 3 MOS. 57.0

TOTAL HOURS 388.5

PREVIOUS ACCIDENT RECORD Clear

INJURIES None

D

NAME AND RANK OF OTHER PERSONNEL INJ.

None

Pass Crash

LOCATION USS WOLVERINE

PURPOSE OF FLIGHT Carrier qualification landing C

FLYING OR LANDING CONDITIONS Good

ANALYSIS

Pilot made a normal approach but lost sight of the signal officer and did not see the cut signal and decided to take a wave off, but the plane had settled and as he applied throttle, the aresting hook engaged number six wire, breaking it, then the hook caught number seven wire pulling the hook assembly out of the plane allowing the plane to leave the deck on the port side and plunge into the water. Plane remained afloat long enough to allow the pilot to get clear.

AIRCRAFT CLASS VF (L)

MODEL AND NUMBER F4U-1 #02465

DAMAGE	A	B	C	D	E	M
AIRPLANE	X					
ENG 1	X					
ENG 2						
ENG 3						
ENG 4						
ENG 5						
ENG 6						

REMARKS

Aircraft and engine lost in Lake Michigan. Not recovered to date.

NATURE OF ACCIDENT J1

PERCENTAGE EACH CAUSE

100% PE (50% judgment, 50% technique)

Entered

U. S. NAVY BUREAU OF AERONAUTICS AIRCRAFT TROUBLE ANALYSIS

signal as other aircraft did, she almost seemed to lack wing structure. No matter what direction we passed her, we just could not get a good image defining an aircraft. When we returned on July 31 to video tape her, we saw what we figured was the reason she gave us such images. She was standing on her propeller and her main landing gear at about a 60-degree attitude. Her empennage was broken off, but not visible to us. It seemed to me that her "gull" wings must have caused the sonar signal to deflect rather than return, giving us the odd images. However, she was stunningly beautiful, resting in about 240 feet of water.

After we had recovered the Hellcat, I had been at a loss as to any future funding of aircraft recoveries. One day I was speaking with Pete Spear, a member of the A and T Recovery lift and disassembly team. Pete is an enthusiast of Navy N2S trainers, also known as a Boeing "Stearman." He owns several of them and has kept one in flying condition for decades. Pete had moved to an area of Wisconsin just north of Illinois and was housing his aircraft in a hangar at the airport in Kenosha. Also keeping his aircraft at that airport is Chuck Greenhill. Pete felt Mr. Greenhill would have an interest in assisting with the recovery and restoration of Lake Michigan aircraft. It did not take Pete much time to make an introduction for me to Mr. Greenhill.

I had not known of and had never met Chuck, but I quickly learned he was a bit of a superstar in the vintage flying "war bird" aircraft world. He owned several P-51 Mustangs, one which he had "Pvt Chuck Greenhill" stenciled on the side indicating his former U.S. Army rank. He also owned a mint-condition Grumman Goose that he liked to take for landings and take-offs on a local river, and a World War II combat veteran Grumman Duck that he had fully restored to flying condition after it had spent years underwater in a Bahamian lagoon. Along with all that, he was a very successful

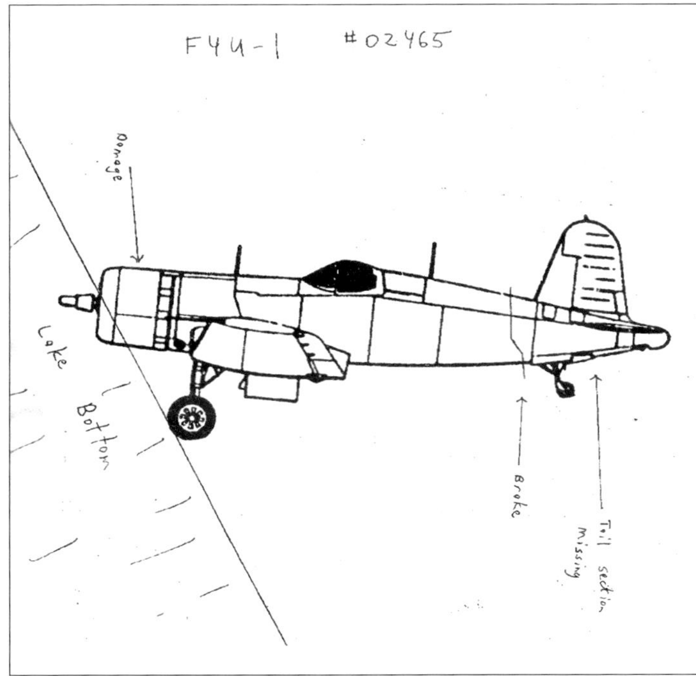

Taras Lyssenko's crash diagram showing the "Bird Cage" Corsair as she sat on the lake's floor.

businessman who had taken a small fabrication shop to a company employing hundreds of people. Upon calling him, I must have said the correct thing for he told me right away that he was interested in becoming involved with the recovery and restoration efforts. It was not long before we all packed into Chuck's private jet and took a trip down to Pensacola in order to meet with Capt. Rasmussen, Capt. Ellis, and Buddy Macon. The results of that meeting was the start of the process to recover Vought F4U-1 "Bird Cage" Corsair, 02465.

After several months of discussions between The National Naval Aviation Museum and the Illinois Historic Preservation Agency, a "Letter of Agreement" was put in place for the aircraft's recovery and restoration. From what I have observed of these "letters," they are very simple with clauses that allow the States input and comments about how the aircraft should be restored and publicly displayed. We had the Army Corps' permit and the other paperwork long before the National Naval Aviation Museum and the Illinois Historic Preservation Agency letter was signed. In the beginning of November 2010, we began our recovery operations.

The wonderful thing was that the recovery of the aircraft was for the most part uneventful aside from a sling chafing on the final lift. It snapped, but the aircraft and crane did not move. After a quick replacement of both slings, we completed the lift and disassembled and shipped her to the National Naval Aviation Museum for rework. "Rework" is the term that Capt. Rasmussen uses for restoration work.

Beginning of the lift of F4U-1 Corsair, 02465. Notice the yellow-colored slings.

A and T Recovery divers Keith Pearson and Bruce Bittner replacing the slings after the port sling chaffed and snapped.

Lift resumes with a new set of slings. Notice the green color. Keith Pearson, Allan Olson, and Bruce Bittner spectate from the deck of A and T Recovery's vessel.

The Corsair almost completely out of the water, but still draining. Notice the quagga mussels on the wing underside.

The lift of F4U-1 almost complete. A and T Recovery archeologist John T Dorwin, Ph.D., patiently awaits his opportunity to inspect the aircraft.

The instrument panel of the Lake Michigan Corsair just after recovery.

Group photograph of Mr. and Mrs. Charles Greenhill, Navy volunteers from Naval Station Great Lakes, Mr. Greenhill's staff, the lift team from Larsen marine, and A and T Recovery crew just after lift out of F4U-1 "Bird Cage" Corsair, 02465.

Todd Brown of A and T Recovery completing disassembly of the Corsair in preparation for transport.

The truck loading of the F4U-1.

20
Air Zoo Aircraft

SBD-2P what?

A short time after we recovered the "Bird Cage" Corsair, Chuck Greenhill asked me if there were other aircraft that we should recover. The answer is that there are always aircraft we should recover and that I had two in mind, a Dauntless and a Wildcat. In the beginning of 2011, I presented to Capt. Rasmussen that Chuck was willing to fund another recovery and I started the permitting process for both aircraft. It should be noted that the approval process in Illinois has always gone relatively smoothly. Our permit applications to the Chicago District Office of the Army Corps of Engineers always seem to end up on the desk of Kathleen Cherich, who is a complete joy to work with, it seems that she really likes the projects. A and T Recovery has had a long track record of dealing with the Illinois Historic Preservation Agency, since the 1980s, so our requests are almost routine. The permitting process started out to be very uneventful. On March 15, 2011, Kathleen sent a letter to Capt. Rasmussen that stated:

> The U.S. Army Corps of Engineers, Chicago District, has completed its review of your notification for authorization under the Regional Permit Program (RPP), submitted on your behalf by A. and T. Recovery, L.L.C. This office has verified that your proposed activity complies with the terms and conditions of Regional Permit #7, "Temporary Construction Activities", and Regional Permit #11, :Marine Structures and Activities:, and the overall RPP under Category 1 of the Regional Permit Program dated April 1, 2007. The activity may be performed without further authorization from this office provided the activity is conducted in compliance with the terms and conditions of the RPP.

It was my hope that we would recover at least one of the aircraft that summer, but as always, bureaucratic delays started to occur. By August, it became clear that we would not be conducting any recoveries because of a very specific reason. From August 15–23, the Navy's Office of Inspector General conducted a "command inspection" of the Naval

History and Heritage Command. For everyone that does not know, true bureaucracies within the U.S. Government seem to come to a grinding halt as soon as they are placed under a microscope. We soon realized that Naval History and Heritage Command's upper staff were going to spend the next six months doing little more than wringing their hands. On December 1, 2011, the Naval Inspector General presented their report to the Navy's command. We would not see what was in the report for about six more months.

As a result of the fallout from the inspection and report on May 24, 2012, Capt. Henry J. Hendrix II was put in place as Director at the Naval History and Heritage Command. It seemed very strange to me that the Head of the Underwater Archeological Branch was not replaced. The report stated:

> P. Dive Program. NAVHISTHERITAGECOM's dive program to conduct underwater archeology, is not operating in accordance with OPNAVINST 3150.27. All diving operations should be suspended until the program is either brought into compliance or a waiver is approved by CNO (OPNAV N87).

The person in charge of that was the same person that a few years earlier, when discussing with the media about A and T Recovery's efforts to rescue the aircraft, made the insane statement: "Think how much more important it will be to recover one in 100 years from now, or 150 years from now, once this generation has died."

Soon after Capt. Hendrix took over at the Naval History and Heritage Command, Capt. Rasmussen made the decision that we should recover the FM-2 Wildcat, 57039. However, the Head of Underwater Archeology Branch had some ideas of how to obstruct. He made the claim that we needed to conduct a "NEPA" (National Environmental Policy Act) study. We had never considered such a study. It had always been our understanding that a NEPA study was needed for large-scale projects, such as the Navy wanting to build a new air base on some island that is the only home to an endangered bird. All we are doing is recovering a small aircraft from the bottom of a lake. On any given summer day, boats sink in that same lake and are recovered without any environmental analysis. Capt. Hendrix being new to the position was not going to override his staff person no matter how nonsensible the demand would be. We would have to conduct the NEPA analysis.

Capt. Rasmussen and I set out to try to comply with the NEPA, while Capt. Hendrix started telling me that if the Illinois Historic Preservation Agency would say our recovery of the aircraft had no "adverse impacts," as they had done years earlier, the study would not be needed. It was clear to everyone that would not happen with the Head of the Underwater Archeology Branch in the conversation. The Navy's newly appointed legal counsel for the Naval History and Heritage Command wasted months proving he was completely inept by not being able to figure out how a NEPA study should be conducted. Everything came to a grinding halt until one day when Capt. Ellis and I were discussing the subject. He mentioned that he had such a study done on one of his projects. He told me that the Naval Facilities Engineering Command were the people he had used. I hung up, put "Naval Facilities Engineering Command Great Lakes" into Google, and within minutes I was on the phone with people who knew who we were at A and T Recovery. They volunteered to complete the NEPA for us on FM-2 Wildcat, 57039. Several months later, in November, we were ready to begin recovery.

The Head of the Underwater Archeological Branch conceived another method of interference. For some reason, he suddenly learned of a thing called "radium." Radium is a radioactive element that was used for many years in paints to illuminate the hands and dials on aircraft instruments. It had been very harmful to employees who worked in factories where they would lick tiny brushes to gain fine points in order to apply the paints to very small surfaces. Every day they worked, those employees would ingest a lot of the radioactive material. It causes cancer when ingested, but it is otherwise harmless. Many years ago, people who deal with historic military aircraft had learned how to handle the instruments that still contained the material, it is removed and replaced with non-radioactive paints. It took about a week for the Navy's environmental people to get over their collective loss of common sense, the Wildcat's recovery continued, with two parting shots. The first was that Capt. Hendrix issued an order that no Navy personnel were to assist with crowd control during the lift. The second was that someone from the Naval History and Heritage Command's staff telephoned the Illinois Emergency Management Agency to tell them that A and T Recovery would be recovering a radioactive aircraft. We went ahead with the recovery. On December 7, 2012 (Pearl Harbor Day), we lifted the aircraft. Being the day it was, the media coverage was almost overwhelming.

During the years prior to the recovery of FM-2 Wildcat, 57039, another problem had developed. The upper staff at the Naval History and Heritage Command had forced a shutdown of the restoration facilities at the National Naval Aviation Museum. Apparently there were some "environmental" issues. It is my understanding that prior to being used for the Museum's restoration efforts, the facility had been used for other Navy purposes that may have left residues of some heavy metals. Over about year, a timeframe with a great amount of money being spent, a massive cleaning was performed, the floor was coated with some sort of shiny epoxy paint, and a good number of restoration volunteers quit. This left us in a position without a place to send the aircraft. Chuck Greenhill stepped forward again, providing us with a small hangar at Kenosha, Wisconsin, which proved to be very beneficial. Throughout the winter of 2012–2013, all sorts of groups, such as Boy Scouts Troops, were able to visit and have an up close look at FM-2 Wildcat, 57039.

Although the hangar had provided us with a temporary storage facility, we were still in a bind as to restoration. During a conversation in the spring of 2013, Capt. Rasmussen asked if I had any relationship with the staff at the Kalamazoo Air Zoo. Its actual name is the Kalamazoo Aviation History Museum. At one time, they had been known for their collection of Grumman "Cat" fighters, therefore "Air Zoo." His idea was to see if they had any interest in restoring the Wildcat. In 1993, we had recovered and sent them a SBD-3 Dauntless, 06624, which they had restored magnificently. Although I live about an hour's car ride from the museum, I had not been there in many years. I told the captain I would contact them and find out their interest level.

I soon found out that the manager of restoration and maintenance, Greg Ward, who had managed the SBD-3 restoration was still employed at the Air Zoo. However, they had a new CEO, Troy Thrash. It took little time before the three of us and a few others piled into an aircraft owned and flown by one of the Air Zoo's volunteers to go take a look at the FM. To me, the Wildcat looked really rough, but there seems to be unified mental phenomena that exists with all people who enjoy the restoration of old things,

Above and below: Lift photographs of FM-2 Wildcat, 57039.

Above left: The representative of the Illinois Emergency Management Agency checking for "radiation" leakage and levels just after recovery of the Wildcat.

Above right: Although it appeared to the casual onlooker that Chuck Greenhill was ecstatic to sit in the cockpit of the just recovered FM-2, we knew that he was actually screaming in extreme pain as a result of the massive dose of radiation he was receiving, not.

Group photograph with Chuck Greenhill recovery sponsor, a Waukegan, Illinois area sixth grade history class that came to view the lift of the Wildcat, and Marine Corps volunteers that assisted with public relations. I guess the Marine Corps' people did not receive the Capt. Hendrix order. (*Photograph courtesy of Mark Russell*)

Above and below: SBD-3 Dauntless, 06624, during recovery lift. Note the impact damage to the wings and engine cowling.

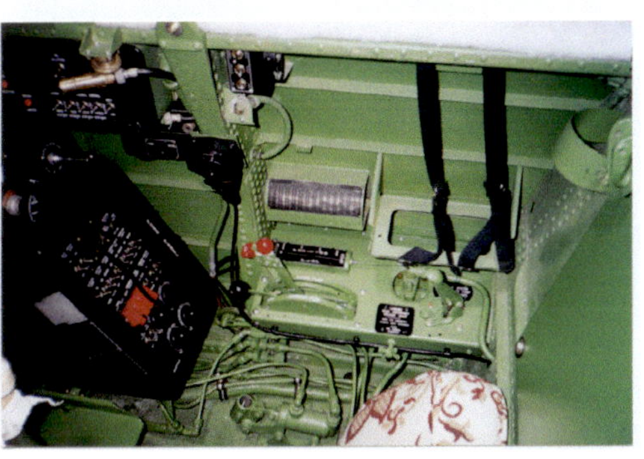

Right: The pilot's cockpit before and after restoration at the Kalamazoo Air Zoo. Note the detailed workmanship.

Below: SBD-3 Dauntless, 06624, restoration completed and ready for public unveiling and display.

the worse it is, the more beautiful it appears to them. The restoration team expressed an interest in tackling the project.

There would be several months of discussions and paperwork completion before the aircraft could be brought to the Air Zoo, but those activities facilitated something we had wished to do for a long time. We wanted to bring a newly recovered aircraft to one of the yearly airshows at Oshkosh, Wisconsin. The Experimental Aircraft Association's Airventures 2013 would soon be held and we would bring this FM-2. Additionally, somewhere in all the conversations about what should be done with this aircraft, an idea to make it an educational project was solidified. At the air show, Troy Thrash, Ed Ellis, and I gave about 100 short presentations of how this FM-2 would not only be restored, but used to educate youth and other members of the American public about the aircraft, the "Greatest Generation," the history of U.S. Navy aviation, along with science, math, engineering, and other technological things.

Seven years before Betsy DeVos became the U.S. Secretary of Education, she and her husband, Richard, founded the West Michigan Aviation Academy in Grand Rapids, Michigan. The mission of the academy is to provide a unique opportunity to explore high school education through a progressive and cutting-edge aviation program, an advanced and multi-faceted engineering curriculum, a caring, inquisitive, and passionate teaching staff. On November 8, 2013, I sent Dick and Betsy DeVos a letter in which I stated:

Shortly after arrival at the Kalamazoo Air Zoo, the main components of FM-2 Wildcat, 57039, are laid out in preparation for disassembly and photo-documentation. (*Photograph courtesy of Tony Sacketos*)

> This past year we retrieved an Eastern Aircraft Division, of General Motors, FM-2 Wildcat Fighter. The aircraft has been brought to the Kalamazoo Aviation History Museum (http://www.airzoo.org/) for restoration. The locating and recovery of the aircraft were funded by Chuck Greenhill. I know the West Michigan Aviation Academy does interact with the Kalamazoo Aviation History Museum, but we have now provided a real education opportunity with the restoration project of this aircraft. I would like for you please look at this project and possibly become involved.

They must have liked what I was proposing. The school's administration contacted me requesting a presentation of what Troy, Greg, and I were thinking. Our presentations to the student body, some insurance policy adjustments, the buy-in from the rest of the restoration staff of the Air Zoo, and soon high school students from the West Michigan Aviation Academy would be working to assist in the restoration of the FM-2 Wildcat, 57039. The project would soon expand to other high schools and Western Michigan University.

In early 2016, I received a call from Capt. Ellis where he explained to me that nothing had happened with the restoration of SBD-2P Dauntless, 2173. The aircraft had also been a victim of the restoration facility shut down at Pensacola. For the past seven years, it had sat almost completely dormant in storage. The Naval Aviation Museum Foundation was under contract to complete the restoration, which had been funded by Fred Turner. Capt. Ellis was seeking my opinion on their situation, to which I replied "Air Zoo."

On July, 1, 2016, after spending the prior day and night on my front lawn, Dauntless SBD-2P, 2173, was delivered, with much fanfare, to the restoration team at the Air Zoo. I was given the opportunity to make a speech:

> Years ago when we at A and T Recovery were out on Lake Michigan looking for the lost Navy World War II aircraft, we were doing it just because we knew there was a demand from museums that wished to display them to the public. We, at least I, did not really give much thought to the human side of the aircraft. Years later I met Fred Turner, McDonald's Honorary Chairman and Former CEO for the corporation.
>
> He had made it possible for the Wildcat we had recovered to go on display at O'Hare International Airport and was working with me and others to locate an SBD Dauntless at Midway International Airport. Later, he would fund the recovery and restoration of the Dauntless that has been brought here today.
>
> I wondered why he had such passion for recovering and restoring these aircraft?
>
> Fred had invited me to visit him at the McDonald's Corporate Headquarters. After he showed me some of the interesting things in his office, he told me some interesting stories. His most important story was how he and Ray Kroc had become friends with Navy pilots that had fought in World War II and other wars. My recollection of his story was that Fred, Ray Kroc and the Navy pilots were part of a club that met annually.
>
> To the Navy pilots, Ray Kroc and Fred Turner were two guys that took a hamburger stand concept and grew it to one of the largest international companies in the world, very impressive.

West Michigan Aviation Academy students disassembling the FM-2 Wildcat's R-1820 engine.

West Michigan Aviation Academy students preforming detail restoration work on the FM-2's wing structure in preparation for the installation of a restored outer skin.

Frontal view of FM-2 Wildcat, 57039, in position within Air Zoo volunteer designed and built fuselage jig.

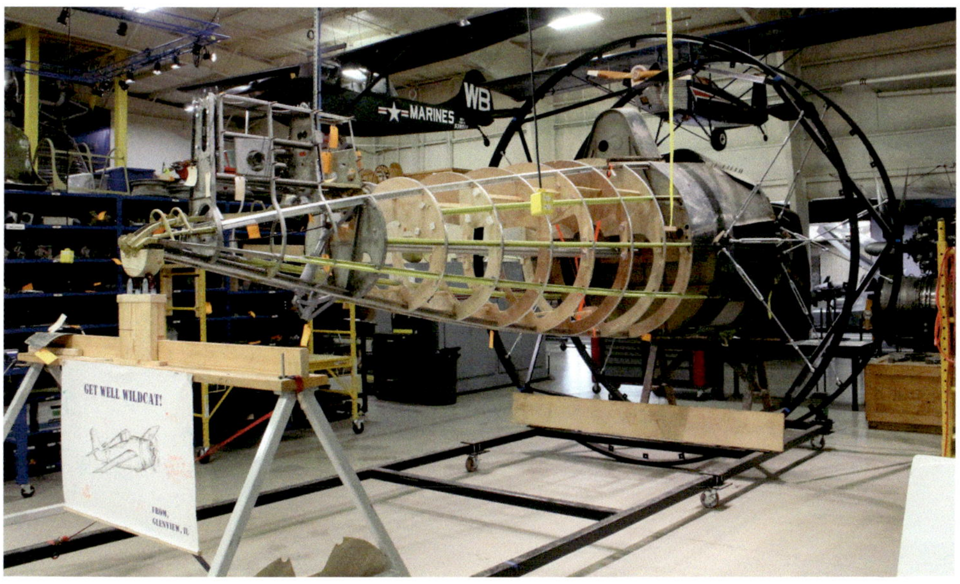

Aft view of FM-2 Wildcat within jig. Note that the empennage section has been reattached to the airframe. It has been over seventy-three years since this aircraft's airframe has been intact and in one piece.

To Ray and Fred, the pilots were the greatest American heroes that ever lived, it was their heroism and that of the Greatest Generation that protected America's and the world's freedom and liberty, providing an environment that allowed them to build a company, McDonald's, into what we know it to be today. In honor of those pilots, Fred and McDonald's sponsored the aircraft projects.

So today, I, we of A and T Recovery wish to thank Fred and McDonald's, those World War II pilots, the Men and Women of the Greatest Generation, Douglas Aircraft (Boeing), the Air Zoo, the Pacific Aviation Museum, the Naval History and Heritage Command, the National Naval Aviation Museum, their Foundation, the aircraft restorers, the students of West Michigan Aviation Academy, everyone else that has been and will be part of this Dauntless project, and all of you for allowing us the honor and privilege to be part of something that has and will touch so many of our lives. Together we all are doing a really good thing.

Thank you, thank you.

The restoration of both aircraft is expected to be completed in 2020.

SBD-2P Dauntless, 2173, just after arrival at the Kalamazoo Air Zoo. Note the really good condition of this aircraft.

A student removing years of Lake Michigan sediment within the tight quarters of the SBD's empennage.

An Air Zoo volunteer supervising a young student during the assembly of the restored engine of SBD-2P Dauntless, 2173.

A volunteer preforming fine detail restoration on the Dauntless.

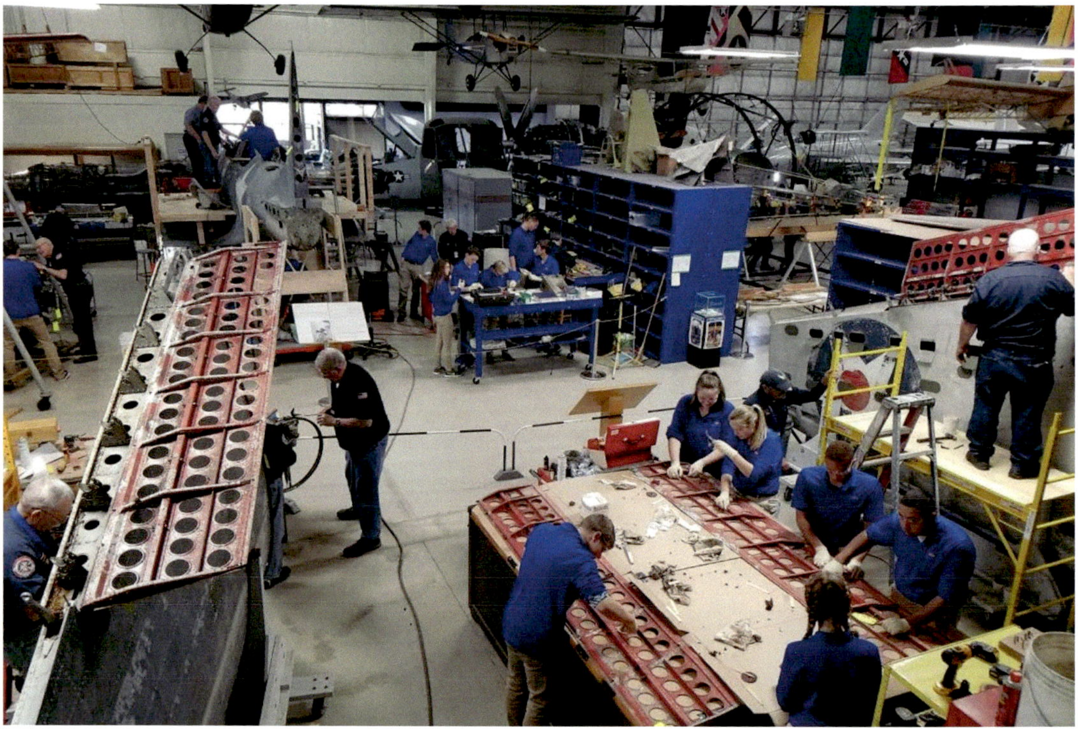

The restoration bays at the Kalamazoo Air Zoo. A vibrant dynamic environment filled with eager students and dedicated volunteers.

21

The *Wells Burt*, *Thomas Hume*, and a Few Other Shipwrecks

There sure are a lot of shipwrecks down there.

During the 1800s, Chicago was one of the busiest ports in the world. By 1871, when the Great Chicago Fire occurred, it had become a major hub of commerce, with dozens of rail lines heading out from the city. After the fire, the city rebuilt quickly. Over the next thirty years, the population grew over five times from nearly 300,000 to almost 1.7 million. Great numbers of sailing and steam vessels brought materials to construct buildings that followed newly implemented codes. As a result of the often-violent weather of the Great Lakes, many of the ships ended up on the bottom of the Southern Basin of Lake Michigan. We at A and T Recovery have located many of these ships in the process of searching for lost aircraft.

The first notable shipwreck find attributed to A and T Recovery was that of the *Wings of the Wind*. In reality, Al was out searching by himself with a low-grade, easy-to-handle side-scan sonar system. We learned something from the find, which was to be careful who you tell. Our policy has always been if someone honors you with sharing their find, the disposition of that find is theirs to determine. In the case of the *Wings of the Wind*, we told a few people where she was and they told sport divers who stripped the wreck site of almost everything possible. It would be the last time we would be so loose with the location of any wreck position.

Several years later, we located the *Wells Burt*. This was the only ship that we located, other than the *UC-97*, which we actually sought to find. Finding her was another one of those things Al just wanted to do. One day, June 28, 1988, he said to me: "... let's go find the *Wells Burt*." So he, Scott, and I went and found her off of Evanston, Illinois. What was amazing to us about this shipwreck was how intact she was being in such shallow water, about 40 feet deep. Her hull was still together and not beaten down by a century of storms. Anything that was missing from the ship was as a result of her salvage shortly after sinking. Being in shallow water, the masts of the ship would have been sticking up from the water and visible to crews of other vessels. After her anchors, masts, other useful ship's equipment were removed by an 1800s salvage team, the position of the wreck site became unknown. After we located her, we turned her location over to the Chicago Maritime Society for their divers to survey, conduct a detailed historical study, and present what they learned to the public.

Several years later, on July 25, 1995, we came across what many believe to be the *Thomas Hume*. Unlike the wreck of the *Wells Burt*, the *Thomas Hume* is in much deeper water. She disappeared in a terrific storm with all of her crew, last seen by the crew of the vessel *Rouse Simmons*. We at A and T Recovery term this sort of shipwreck as a “sail-away,” because no one really has a clue where to look for the ship.

The *St. Marys*, *Wells Burt*, and the *Thomas Hume* were all Great Lakes schooners. A schooner is a sailing vessel with a certain configuration of its sails. The *St. Marys* was another sail-away that had gone missing the same evening another infamous Great Lakes’ disaster had occurred, the collision and sinking of the *Lady Elgin*. That tragedy greatly over shadowed the loss of the *St. Marys*. She faded from historical knowledge. We came across her in about 110 feet of water.

The *Rotarian* had been a ship that was moored in the Chicago River where she had been used as a restaurant and night club. She sank at her dock, was raised, then towed out into the lake and scuttled. Scuttling off the shore of Chicago was a common way old, worn-out ships were disposed of for many years. We located the ship along with many others that litter the floor of Lake Michigan.

A row of “dead eyes” of the *Wells Burt*. (*Photograph courtesy of Michele Hagerman*)

Some of the deck hardware of the *Wells Burt* showing many years of damage done by Lake Michigan storms. Notice that Lake Michigan shallow water visibly is not always clear. (*Photograph courtesy of Michele Hagerman*)

What was once a section of the deck of the *Wells Burt*. In the photograph, a ship's capstan can be seen. (*Photograph courtesy of Michele Hagerman*)

Another view of dead eyes along with "belaying" pins of the *Wells Burt*. (*Photograph courtesy of Keith Pearson*)

The bow of the shipwreck *Thomas Hume*. (*Photograph courtesy of Mike Pedersen*)

The stern of the shipwreck *Thomas Hume*. (*Photograph courtesy of Mike Pedersen*)

The deck of the shipwreck *Thomas Hume*. (*Photograph courtesy of Mike Pedersen*)

The *St. Marys*, as with many other wooden shipwrecks, has been badly beaten down over the many years on the lake's floor. In the photograph, a ship's windless and anchor are visible. (*Photograph courtesy of Mike Pedersen*).

22

SBD-1 Bureau Number 1612

You were cold and alone, but we will never again let you be forgotten.

In early 2016, I was contacted by members of the Flying Leathernecks Historical Foundation. Their hope was that I would be willing to come and make a presentation at their annual gala. My talk was to be about the locating and recovery of the SBD-1 Dauntless, 1612, which they were working to restore. A short time later, they informed me that my speaking engagement would be delayed for a year because the former California Governor Pete Wilson was going to speak that year. It was fine with me because I was a bit confused. My recollection was that we had shipped that Dauntless to the U.S.S. *Alabama* Battleship Memorial Park.

I began doing research on the aircraft, its history and the history of the pilot who had last flown her, in preparation for my presentation, which had been rescheduled for May 2017. What I would find was a cost of war that seems to be so seldom known and understood by those other than the people who are directly affected. I once heard it said, "to truly know the pain of war one must understand that when the life of a young man is taken it is not only he who has lost greatly. There are many who loved him, they suffer terribly as well."

The history of 1612 was actually very linear and easy to follow. The aircraft is a Dauntless SBD-1, of which there had been only fifty-seven built. Although it does not appear the aircraft was involved in any combat action, for a brief period of time during 1942, it was assigned to Marine Scout Bombing Squadron 142 (VMSB-142).

In August 1942, she was assigned to the Carrier Qualification Training Unit at Glenview Naval Air Station. On November 21, 1942, she was lost in Lake Michigan along with her pilot Ensign Herbert Welton McMinn of Gouldbusk, Texas. After recovery by A and T Recovery in early 1994, she was placed on loan to the U.S.S. *Alabama* Battleship Memorial Park for major restoration and static display. The National Museum of Naval Aviation requested return of the aircraft stating, "it has been designated for another project..." Then the National Museum of Naval Aviation loaned the Dauntless to the San Diego Carrier Museum for restoration for a period of fifteen

The World War II emblem of Marine Scout Bombing Squadron 142 (VMSB-142).

years. In 2012, the San Diego Carrier Museum, now named the U.S.S. *Midway* Museum transferred the aircraft to the Flying Leathernecks Museum, where it is on loan from the National Naval Aviation Museum for a period of fifteen years (May 23, 2012 to June 1, 2027). She is still undergoing restoration.

For my presentation, I really wanted to tell something of the pilot, for the aircraft is a machine, but the pilots are men who had lives full of hope, fear, joy, pain, and love. This pilot's life was cut so short, people should know something of him. I collected all the information I could from the college he had attended, Texas A&M, and the Naval History and Heritage Command. I enlisted the assistance of David Hardin, archivist (RL-SL), the National Personnel Records Center, the National Achieves, St. Louis, Missouri. David Hardin was able to locate hundreds of pages of training documents and other records that detailed almost everything Ensign McMinn had done in his life. I started to focus on several of the Navy's documents I found in the personnel records that were from the time of the loss of Ensign McMinn and the SBD.

A document drafted on December 2, 1942 was from the CO of the Carrier Qualification Training Unit, Glenview, Illinois, reporting to the Secretary of the Navy, Office of the Judge Advocate General, via the Chief of Air Operational Training and the Chief of the Bureau of Naval Personnel, it stated:

> 3. Ensign McMinn was observed by a civilian, Mr. Albert Kleist, whose statement is forwarded herewith as Enclosure (A), to land in Lake Michigan about five (5) miles offshore on November 21, 1942, on which day the water temperature was forty-two (42) degrees Fahrenheit and the wind eighteen (18) knots from the northeast. To date neither the body nor the plane have been recovered but dragging operations are still in progress.

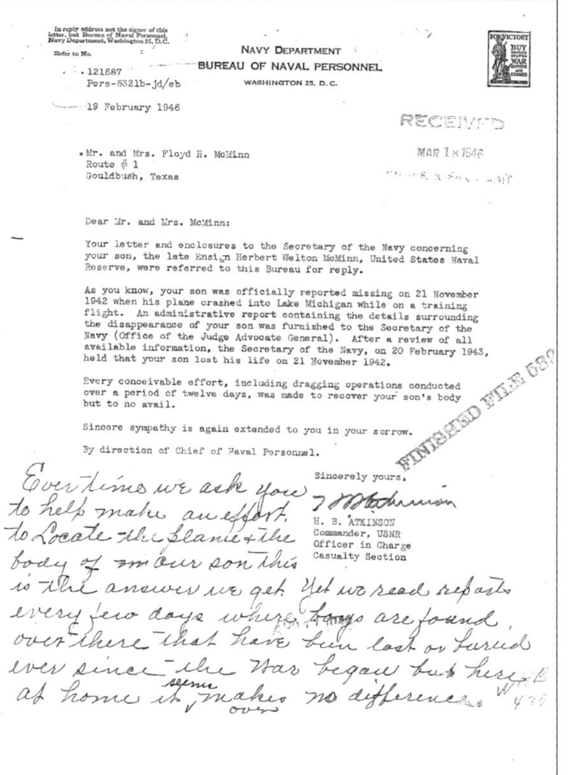

In reply address not the signer of this letter, but Bureau of Naval Personnel, Navy Department, Washington 25, D.C.

Refer to No.
121687
Pers-5321b-jd/eb

NAVY DEPARTMENT
BUREAU OF NAVAL PERSONNEL
WASHINGTON 25, D.C.

19 February 1946

RECEIVED
MAR 1 1946

Mr. and Mrs. Floyd H. McMinn
Route # 1
Gouldbush, Texas

Dear Mr. and Mrs. McMinn:

Your letter and enclosures to the Secretary of the Navy concerning your son, the late Ensign Herbert Welton McMinn, United States Naval Reserve, were referred to this Bureau for reply.

As you know, your son was officially reported missing on 21 November 1942 when his plane crashed into Lake Michigan while on a training flight. An administrative report containing the details surrounding the disappearance of your son was furnished to the Secretary of the Navy (Office of the Judge Advocate General). After a review of all available information, the Secretary of the Navy, on 20 February 1943, held that your son lost his life on 21 November 1942.

Every conceivable effort, including dragging operations conducted over a period of twelve days, was made to recover your son's body but to no avail.

Sincere sympathy is again extended to you in your sorrow.

By direction of Chief of Naval Personnel.

Sincerely yours,

H. B. ATKINSON
Commander, USNR
Officer in Charge
Casualty Section

FINISHED FILE

Ever times we ask you to help make an effort to Locate the plane & the body of our son this is the answer we get. Yet we read reports every few days where boys are found over there that have been lost or buried ever since the War began but here at home it seems makes no difference. over

2

if they are never found. There was perhaps a feable effort made to find our boy, too busy too much trouble, he was not your son. We have worked hard all through this war helped the Red Cross and have baught all the bonds we could but now we are through. if our effort was in vain, and we get no help when we beg for it. It was through neglect that our dear boy lost his life from all avaliable information we have been given prove this. beyond a doubt. If you big boys in the office had to take our place for a while you would try in some way to help. We're sure the Seatary of Navy never saw the letter we wrote him or he would have at least answered it. No need to ask or beg of you again to make another effort to help us. We've ask and prayed that he might be found (dead or a live) If this were you son, how would you feel?

Mr + Mrs F. H. McMinn.

These letters show the pain this family endured.

I would learn from other documents that had been drafted on later dates that the Navy had spent twelve days dragging the lake floor in an attempt to locate the Dauntless. They just did not have the sonar technology at the time to locate the submerged aircraft. More importantly, in those documents, I saw the grief of a family who sought answers and would not give up on having something of their son returned.

In preparing my presentation for the Flying Leathernecks' Foundation gala, I searched for the family of the pilot. It was my wish that they could participate or at least provide me with some statements for my audience. The modern internet is a wonderful thing. I located a 1940 census document that provided me with the names of those who were in the McMinn family household at the time. The family consisted of Floyd H. McMinn (aged fifty-five); his wife, Jewell McMinn (aged fifty-three); daughter, Thelma Lynch (aged thirty); her son, Joe Floyd Lynch (aged seven); and Herbert Welton McMinn (aged twenty-one). The family member I focused on was Joe Floyd Lynch, I believed that he had the most likely chance of still being alive. What I found was an obituary for Joe Floyd Lynch, he has passed away February 17, 2014. In the write-up, it stated that Joe Lynch had also been a U.S. Navy aviator, a pilot of a P2V Neptune. There was a photograph of him and to me he looked a lot like Ensign McMinn. The obituary also told me that Mr. Lynch was survived by his sons and their families: Bryan and Angela

Lynch, Laura and Cameron; Brad and Ginger Lynch, Kyle, Sam, and Owen; and David and Christina Lynch. However, when I contacted the staff at the funeral home, they refused to assist me in my attempts to reach any member of the family. They would not even give family members my contact information. I was momentarily stalled.

I gave my presentation for the Flying Leathernecks' Historical Foundation, but I was not finished. I really wanted to find Ensign McMinn's family. It seemed to me that they should know what had happened, it was their story. My search led me to the website LinkedIn where I found a Bryan Lynch, Chief Technology Officer, at Reliant Heart. I sent him a request to "connect." On June 28, 2017, Bryan Lynch responded by accepting my connection request. I promptly sent him a note, "Hello, Was your father Joe Floyd Lynch, your grandmother Thelma Lynch Bounds, your great grandfather Floyd McMinn, great grandmother Jewel McMinn? If so I have a story to tell you that you will want to hear."

He very quickly sent back: "That's me. How do you know them?"

I told him the story, to which he responded: "Wow! I had no idea! Let me review this for a few minutes.... I have several possessions of my dad's uncle Herbert including his violin. My dad, Joe, passed away in 2014. My brothers will be excited."

I do not know if our recovery of SBD-1 Dauntless, 1612, has brought the McMinn family any peace. For so long, I have heard the word "closure" used in such situations. I also do not know if it that really applies in this situation. What I do know is that in 1994, Capt. Rasmussen, Buddy Macon, the staff at the National Aviation Museum Foundation, and those of us at A and T Recovery did something that showed that the life of one person who died cold and alone had meaning. There are cultures in this world that believe that a person's spirit remains on earth with us as long as their name is spoken. Ensign McMinn's name will be remembered and spoken for a long, long time. At A and T Recovery, we say the aircraft have a "circle of life" of which we are just a small part. We are glad that we played our role well in this aircraft's circle of life.

Right: The official U.S. Navy photograph of Ensign Herbert Welton McMinn, U.S. Naval Reserve.

Below: Taras Lyssenko, Bryan Lynch, and restorer Robert Cramise viewing SBD-1 Dauntless, 1612. (*Photograph courtesy of C. J. Machado*)

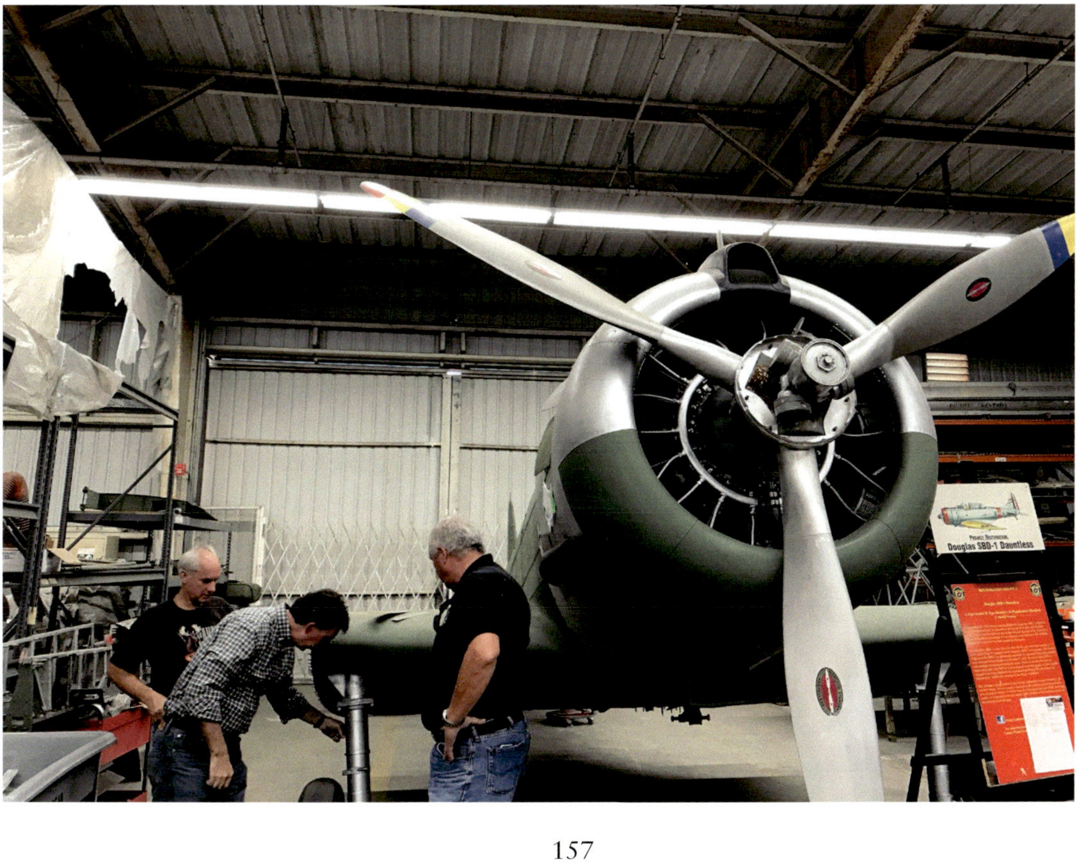

Bryan Lynch viewing SBD-1 Dauntless, 1612, under restoration at the Flying Leatherneck Aviation Museum, Marine Corps Air Station Miramar, San Diego, California. (*Photograph courtesy of C. J. Machado*)

23

A Never Ending Story

I do not believe we are finished.

For those of us at A and T Recovery, it has been a privilege, honor, and pleasure to have been able to be a small part of the grand effort to recover, restore, and present to the public the once lost World War II U.S. Navy aircraft of Lake Michigan. We will always know that we were able to overcome the ill will and misdeeds of the handful of misguided individuals who always sought to thwart the effort. For the thousands of people who participated, they and we know what we achieved will be a positive part of the world as long as our society exists. Together we have brought forth inspirational benefit to the tens of millions of people who have and will be able to see and learn from these aircraft for many generations to come. It is our hope that what we have done helped to always preserve the knowledge and memory of the "Greatest Generation" for it is they who made the true sacrifices in order to preserve the world's freedom and liberty.

Let it be known that we are not finished and there are still aircraft that need to be rescued. Hopefully others will join us on this quest that has many years before it will end.

Acknowledgments

As author, I wish to thank the thousands of people that made the rescue, restoration, and presentation to the public of the once lost World War II U.S. Navy aircraft of Lake Michigan possible.

Thanks to editor Debra Haight, and to Capt. Robert Rasmussen, U.S.N. (Ret.), and Capt, Charles "Ed" Ellis, U.S.N. (Ret.), who provided content and factual verification.